WAS THERE A "GOVERNMENT CONNECTION"?

"The police and press . . . never took him seriously, even after the bombing of our home. They said he did it himself. Now what are they going to do—say that he shot himself?"—Betty Shabazz

New York police knew weeks in advance that Malcolm was an assassination target. They had at least one undercover agent in his organization, and a wiretap on his phone. But no police were in sight at the Audubon Ballroom when Malcolm was killed.

"Prevent the *rise of a 'messiah'* who could unify, and electrify, the militant black nationalist movement. [Malcolm X] might have been such a 'messiah;' he is the martyr of the movement today."—J. Edgar Hoover (secret memorandum) March 4, 1968

The FBI has been implicated in the assassinations of Black Panther leaders Fred Hampton and Mark Clark, and a campaign to "get" Martin Luther King. The CIA has organized plots to assassinate Fidel Castro and Patrice Lumumba.

Were local and federal police involved in the assassination of Malcolm X?

D1042932

CIVIC CENTER

The Assassination of
Malcolm X

THE
MILITANT

NEWS ABOUT:

BLACK NATIONALISM

CIVIL RIGHTS

COLONIAL

REVOLUTION

ON SALE HERE

The Assassination of
Malcolm X

George Breitman, Herman Porter, and Baxter Smith

PATHFINDER

New York   London   Toronto   Sydney

Copyright © 1976, 1991 by Pathfinder Press

ISBN 978-0-87348-632-3
Library of Congress Catalog Card Number 76-47347
Manufactured in Canada

First edition, 1976
Second edition, 1988
Third edition, 1991
Sixth printing, 2008

Cover photo by Robert Parent. Malcolm X at a November 24, 1964, news
conference in New York after his second trip to Africa that year.

Pathfinder
www.pathfinderpress.com
E-mail: pathfinder@pathfinderpress.com

CONTENTS

INTRODUCTION

This book, first published in 1976, is about the assassination of Malcolm X on February 21, 1965. Assessing the known facts, it demonstrates that the official government version of how the assassination occurred is not credible. The evidence points to government complicity in the murder.

The book also takes up the widespread misrepresentation of Malcolm X's ideas since his death. It aims to stimulate the study of his views and a recognition of their importance for effective political action against racism, war, the oppression of women, and the exploitation of working people the world over.

This updated introduction outlines important revelations related to the assassination that have come to light since the book was first issued. An index has also been added to this edition.

Eleven months after the assassination, the Manhattan prosecutor's office brought to trial three men charged with the crime. One, Talmadge Hayer, was caught at the scene. The other two, Norman Butler and Thomas Johnson, known members of the Nation of Islam (also known as the Black Muslims), were arrested soon after. All three are Black.

The government's version of the crime was simple: the three defendants, acting alone, killed Malcolm X. They were said to be motivated by the strife between the Nation of Islam and Malcolm X after he broke from it in March 1964 and formed the Muslim Mosque, Inc., and a few months later the Organization of Afro-American Unity (OAAU). According to the government, that was all there was to it. No one else was involved—neither organized racist groups nor government officials, who hated Malcolm X's revolutionary example and internationalist outlook; nor agents of cop organizations that were surveilling and harassing Malcolm, such as the "antisubversive" squad of the New York City police; nor other Black Muslims being used by government agencies (the most likely scenario).

At the 1966 trial, the interests of the government's various police agencies were all represented by the district attorney. Hayer had his own lawyers and Butler and Johnson were represented by court-appointed attorneys. But no one was allowed to testify on behalf of Malcolm X or his supporters and family, or to ask the questions that could have helped bring the truth to light and all of Malcolm X's killers to justice.

Toward the end of the seven-week trial, Hayer, who denied being a Black Muslim, confessed that he had participated in the killing. He claimed he had been hired to do the job but insisted that Butler and Johnson had not been involved. Neither the district attorney nor the defense attorneys showed much interest in pursuing the identity of the person or persons Hayer said had hired him. All three defendants were convicted and given twenty-year-to-life sentences.

The version peddled by the government and the big-business press was full of contradictions, inconsistencies, and leads not followed up. Many of these contradictions were reported then and subsequently by the *Militant*, a socialist newsweekly. The authors of this book, George Breitman, Herman Porter, and Baxter Smith, were staff writers for the *Militant*, from which most of the material published here is taken. Smith's article in chapter 7 first appeared in the *Black Scholar* in 1974.

In the mid-1960s few people in the United States would have believed that the government would engage in political assassination. That attitude was soon to change. The credibility gap between the government and the U.S. people widened throughout the Vietnam War; millions learned they could not trust Washington. The Watergate cover-up, which forced President Richard Nixon's resignation, taught this lesson to millions more in the mid-1970s. Revelations also came to light about flagrant government conspiracies to organize police murders of Black militants, such as the assassination of Fred Hampton in Chicago in 1969.

New political space opened for working people and opponents of government spying and harassment to strike blows in defense of democratic rights.

Congress was compelled in the mid-1970s to open investigations of the CIA, FBI, and other political police agencies. While the aim was to portray their crimes as isolated abuses now corrected through congressional "oversight" legislation, a substantial amount of information was forced out.

CIA-organized or -assisted plots to overthrow governments (for example, the coup in Chile in 1973) are now well known. So too are its conspiracies to assassinate heads of government, such as the unsuccessful efforts to eliminate Fidel Castro of Cuba, and the U.S.-government-organized murders of Ernesto Che Guevara in Bolivia in 1967 and of Patrice Lumumba of the Congo in 1961. According to a 1975 U.S. Senate report, in 1960 the CIA viewed Lumumba's assassination as "an urgent and prime objective," in the words of then CIA director Allen Dulles. A "reasonable inference" could be made, the Senate report stated, that the order to kill Lumumba came directly from President Dwight Eisenhower.

As workers and peasants engaged in struggles to topple dictatorial regimes such as those of the shah of Iran, Eric Gairy in Grenada, and the Somoza dynasty in Nicaragua in the late 1970s, the truth about the U.S. government's role in backing these repressive dictatorships became more widely known. Washington was caught lying about its arming of South African–backed counterrevolutionaries in Angola, and was shown to be covertly arming the contras to wage a war against the people and government of Nicaragua.

Also well known today are the U.S. rulers' consistent violations of fundamental constitutional rights through burglaries, wiretaps, unauthorized opening of mail, infiltration of organizations, provocations of violence, and training of local police departments on how to commit such crimes on their own.

Lawsuits in the 1970s by the Socialist Workers Party and Young Socialist Alliance, as well as by other organizations and individuals, forced the FBI and other federal government police agencies to turn over hundreds of thousands of pages of previously secret documents. In 1973 the historic suit known as *Socialist Workers Party v. Attorney General* was filed. In the ensuing years thousands of illegal acts by the FBI and its informers were revealed. In 1986 the court found the FBI guilty; the government declined to appeal. The story of this victorious fight and its conquests for the political rights of all is told in two Pathfinder books: *COINTELPRO: The FBI's Secret War on Political Freedom*, by Nelson Blackstock, and *FBI on Trial*, which contains the federal court decision and other documents.

The union movement, communist groups, antiwar coalitions, women's liberation organizations, and solidarity groups such as the Committee in Solidarity with the People of El Salvador have been targets of such government disruption during many decades.

But no target was more prominent than the Black rights movement, especially in the 1960s. Leaders of Black rights organizations were victimized, including not only Malcolm X but also Martin Luther King, Jr., and other figures with a wide variety of political viewpoints. The organizations that came under attack ranged from the NAACP to the Nation of Islam. The FBI even sought to have the Nation prosecuted for subversion in the 1950s under the thought-control Smith Act. Information on government efforts to destroy the Black movement as far back as the Second World War can be found in the article "Washington's Fifty-Year Domestic Contra Operation," by Larry Seigle, in issue 6 of the magazine *New International*, distributed by Pathfinder.

The FBI and CIA claimed that all they were doing was collecting "intelligence" about Black organizations for possible use in the prosecution of lawbreakers. But their true aim was to smash the movement for Black liberation.

This is demonstrated by documents of the FBI's own Counterintelligence Program (COINTELPRO) that were released through the Freedom of Information Act. Some of these are reprinted as an appendix to chapter 7. Dated from 1967 to 1970, they record the government's aim as being "to expose, disrupt, misdirect, discredit, or otherwise neutralize the activities of black nationalist, hate-type organizations and groupings, their leadership, spokesmen, membership, and supporters."

In addition, the FBI's agents were directed to "exploit through counterintelligence techniques the organizational and personal conflicts of the leadership of the groups" and where possible to make an effort to "capitalize upon existing conflicts between competing black nationalist organizations." Also, to "prevent the coalition of militant black nationalist groups . . . and leaders from gaining respectability" and to "prevent the rise of a 'messiah' who could unify, and electrify, the militant black nationalist movement."

In the context of the growing organized opposition in the mid-1960s to Washington's bloody war against the Vietnamese people, the government was also determined to crack down on those such as Malcolm X who spoke out uncompromisingly against U.S. imperialism, its exploitation of peoples throughout the world, and its military interventions and wars.

Carrying out the orders laid out in these FBI directives, paid informers and agents provocateurs were sent into targeted organizations. Among other things, they set these groups up for fratricidal warfare (for example, between the Black Panthers on one side and, on the other, the US organization in California, the Blackstone Rangers in Chicago, etc.). Taken as a whole, these and other files confirm the close ties that the government's political police maintain with local police forces and their antilabor and Red squads, as well as ultrarightist outfits like the Ku Klux Klan.

Developments since the publication of this book in 1976 reinforce the questions raised by its authors.

The doubts about the frame-up case against Butler and Johnson were confirmed in 1977–78 when Hayer, now calling himself Mujahid Halim, filed affidavits through attorney William Kunstler again asserting Butler and Johnson's innocence, but this time naming four other Muslims from New Jersey as his fellow killers. While still insisting the five men acted alone, Hayer admitted in 1979, "Maybe I was manipulated, maybe I was a pawn—I don't know." To this day the government refuses to reopen the case.

Butler, who now calls himself Muhammad Abdul Aziz, was finally released on parole in June 1985, more than twenty years after his incarceration. Johnson, today Khalil Islam, was subsequently paroled as well. Hayer remains in prison.

In 1982 Benjamin Goodman (today Benjamin Karim) told Mike Wallace in a "60 Minutes" show that Butler and Johnson were not present when Malcolm X was assassinated. Goodman, who knew Butler and Johnson, had been on the stage at the time and had thoroughly scanned the audience. Although he testified to a grand jury, he was never called to testify at the trial.

Another significant omission from the witness list was Gene Roberts, one of Malcolm X's bodyguards, who was present at the assassination. In December 1970 Roberts was revealed to have been an undercover cop assigned by the Bureau of Special Services (BOSS), the New York Police Department's Red squad, to infiltrate the OAAU.

In his 1973 biography of Malcolm X (discussed here in chapter 6), Peter Goldman accepted the official story as essentially accurate. While Goldman continued in his second edition in 1979 to affirm that the government was not involved, he was forced to admit that its version was no longer credible.

Since *The Assassination of Malcolm X* was published in 1976, thousands of pages of FBI files on Malcolm X have been forced out into the open. In 1977 the *Militant*, through a Freedom of Information Act request, received the first 1,300 pages of these files. While heavily censored and far from complete, they show that Malcolm X was the subject of one of the most intensive spy operations ever conducted by the FBI. They include everything from detailed reports by informants on OAAU rallies to memos describing the FBI's success in getting a meeting for Malcolm X canceled at a Baltimore high school.

The files are laced with rumors of assassination plots against Malcolm X, yet not one word is included on the plot that ended his life. This despite the fact that the New York police publicly admitted at the time of Malcolm X's death that they knew an attempt was to be made on his life.

In 1978 Scholarly Resources, Inc. published 2,300 pages of FBI files on Malcolm X in a microfilm edition. The earliest file dates from 1953, when he had just become a minister for the Nation of Islam. It notes that he had been placed on the government's notorious Security Index of people to be detained in times of "danger to national security." The files also include reports from FBI informants present at the assassination.

People who charged that the government was out to get Malcolm X were dismissed as "paranoid" twenty-five years ago, but who would dare say that now? Would the government that ordered its agents to "exploit" and "capitalize upon" conflicts among Black militants have refrained from inflaming resentment against Malcolm X among members and leaders of the Nation of Islam? Would it have refrained from inciting them to "neutralize" him?

Would the government that tried to "neutralize" Fidel Castro by killing him and that ordered the assassinations of Che Guevara and Patrice Lumumba have had any scruples against using the same means to prevent the rise of what it termed a "messiah" at home?

Getting to the truth behind the assassination of Malcolm X is not just a matter of historical interest. It is an important weapon in the ongoing fight for freedom for political discussion, organization, and action—without government harassment and disruption. This struggle is vital not only to Blacks but to all workers, unionists, farmers, and fighters for democratic rights and social justice.

And in all these struggles, the ideas and example of Malcolm X—of his revolutionary, internationalist, and anticapitalist course—will be an indispensable political weapon.

Steve Clark
January 1991

DATES, EVENTS, AND QUESTIONS

1964

March 8 — Malcolm X announces his split with the Nation of Islam.

June 28 — Founding of Organization of Afro-American Unity.

Late July — Malcolm hospitalized in Cairo, violently ill, he suspects U.S. agents of poisoning him.

1965

February 9 — Malcolm is barred from France. Did French government expect assassination there? Was U.S. State Department involved in banning Malcolm?

February 14 — Malcolm's house bombed. A whiskey bottle of gasoline appears in children's room during investigation. Police hint Malcolm bombed his own house and family, seeking publicity. Did cops try to frame Malcolm?

February 15 — Malcolm demands FBI investigation, State Department explanation of attacks on him. During his talk at Audubon Ballroom, a scuffle occurs in audience. Was this a rehearsal for the assassination?

February 20 — Malcolm tells associate he will stop saying Muslims are responsible for attacks. Checks into New York Hilton. Several Black men, including one later identified by hotel security officer as Talmadge Hayer, one of accused assassins, ask for Malcolm's room number.

February 21 — As a scuffle in Audubon Ballroom audience draws attention of Malcolm's guards, Malcolm is assassinated. Talmadge Hayer is caught by crowd. A second suspect is reported caught at scene, later disappears from press. Police say "feud" between Malcolm and Muslims led to murder. What role did undercover New York police, wiretap on OAAU phone, play in assassination plot?

February 22 — Police say five or more men assassinated Malcolm. Cops claim 100 of Malcolm's followers are en route to kill Elijah Muhammad. The OAAU denies these reports. Were police trying to start a war between Black organizations?

February 24 — Asst. Chief Inspector Coyle tells reporters police are "on the right track." He says witnesses are being shown photographs, refuses to comment on reports police have motion pictures taken outside Audubon.

February 25 — "A police source confirmed that there are plans to kill Hayer. 'They don't want this guy to testify,' the source said." (N. Y. Journal American) Boston OAAU head Leon 4X Ameer says, "Nobody believed Malcolm X when he said his life was in danger, and now I am in the same predicament."

February 26 — Police arrest Norman 3X Butler, a Fruit of Islam leader already charged in shooting of Benjamin Brown, a former Muslim. Brown comments: "I never knew Butler to carry a gun. . . . After all his trouble over my case, how could he have gone after Malcolm too?" Police still seek three more men.

March 1 — Office of Percy Sutton, Malcolm's lawyer, is burglarized and thoroughly searched. Some Malcolm X papers are stolen. Were government "plumbers" involved?

March 2 — Police pick up Cary Thomas, one of Malcolm's guards, for questioning. After two days with police interrogators, he becomes star witness for the prosecution.

March 3 — Police arrest Thomas 15X Johnson, whom Cary Thomas identifies. Johnson is a former bodyguard of Muhammad Ali, and is codefendant with Butler in another shooting. Cary Thomas is held as material witness until trial, one year later. Police drop the investigation, and stop looking for other suspects.

March 13 — Leon 4X Ameer dies of overdose of sleeping pills in Boston. He has just announced plans to produce tapes and documents of Malcolm's proving the government was responsible for assassination.

1966

January 21 — Assassination trial begins.

February 28 — Hayer confesses, exonerates Butler and Johnson.

March 11 — The three defendants are convicted.

April 14 — Judge sentences Hayer, Butler, and Johnson to life, refuses defense motion to open police files containing notes on interviews with 100 eyewitnesses. Would this hidden evidence have changed outcome of trial?

I

Malcolm X
The man and his ideas

by George Breitman

This speech was given at a meeting of the Friday Night Socialist Forum at Eugene V. Debs Hall, Detroit, on March 5, 1965, twelve days after Malcolm's assassination. Its essential analysis was expanded by Breitman a year later in The Last Year of Malcolm X: The Evolution of a Revolutionary (Pathfinder Press, 1967). The text was first printed in the Militant, March 22 and 29, 1965.

It is still painful to speak of the death of Malcolm X. It is probably too soon to appraise him adequately. It will take time before we can do him justice, before we can see him in his full stature. It is painful because with him gone, we momentarily feel smaller, weaker, more vulnerable.

Our sense of loss is for his family, for the movement he was building, for the Negro people, for the revolutionary cause as a whole. There is also something in us that cries out against the fact that he was cut down in his prime, still a young man, before he had made his full contributions to the struggle, before he had accomplished everything he was capable of accomplishing for human emancipation.

I was still a young man twenty-five years ago when another great revolutionary was assassinated—Leon Trotsky. Perhaps I did not fully realize how much his leadership, advice, and political wisdom would be missed, and probably I was under the influence of the belief common among young people that to show certain kinds of strong emotion is a sign of weakness. Anyhow, I did not cry when Trotsky was killed, but I could not help crying when Malcolm was killed.

It was not because I considered Malcolm the greater of the two men. One reason for the difference was the realization that Malcolm, at the age of thirty-nine, was still in the process of reaching his full height, still in the process of working out his program, still in the early stage of building a new movement—whereas Trotsky, at the age of sixty, had already reached full maturity, had already worked out his main ideas and his program, and left behind him the solid foundations of a movement that could not be destroyed by war, by persecution from both the Allied and Axis powers, or by cold war reaction and witch-hunts.

But while it is painful to speak of Malcolm, and not yet possible to see him in full perspective, we are able even now to begin to make an appraisal of his ideas, and of how he came to the ideas that constitute his heritage. When we do this, we must try to put emotion aside, or to bring it under control. That is what Malcolm urged when he spoke here in Detroit three weeks ago—that we learn to think clearly about the struggle and the ways the power structure seeks to curb and sidetrack the struggle; that we think clearly and rely on reason and learn how to see through trickery.

Malcolm Little's mother was born as the result of her mother's rape by a white man in the West Indies. When Malcolm was four, the house where he and his family lived was burned down by Ku Kluxers. When he was six, his father met a violent death, and he and his family always believed his father had been lynched.

The family was broken up. Young Malcolm lived in state institutions and boarding homes. He got high marks at the grade school in Mason, Michigan. Then, at the age of fifteen, he became a dropout. He went to live with his sister in Boston, and went to work at the kinds of jobs available to Negro youth—shoeshine boy, soda jerk, hotel busboy, member of a dining car crew on trains traveling to New York, restaurant waiter in Harlem. There he drifted into the degrading life of the underworld—gambling, drugs, hustling, burglary. You can find it all described in his autobiography, up to and including his arrest for burglary, conviction, and sentencing to ten years in prison. That was in 1946, when he was not quite twenty-one, the age of many of you in this audience.

What were his ideas then? That life is a jungle, where the fiercest survive—by fleecing the weak and defenseless; where each man looks out for number one, which can only be done by accepting the jungle code. "The main thing you got to remember is that everything in the world is a hustle," he was told by the friend who helped him get his first job.

Although his father had been an admirer of Marcus Garvey, feelings of race pride did not exist in the young man with the zoot suit; he tried to straighten his hair in emulation of white men, who, as he later said, had taught him what he knew and instilled in him the values of racist white society. I think you can find thousands of youngsters in today's ghetto like twenty-one-year-old Malcolm Little in 1946.

Prison is hell. Prison is also a place where you can think, where some important decisions have been made. Eugene V. Debs, after whom this meeting hall is named, was converted to socialism while he was in prison in 1895. Prison was where Malcolm underwent a conversion that literally transformed his whole life.

By letters and visits from members of his family he was introduced to the Nation of Islam, headed by Elijah Muhammad. This American religious sect, popularly known as the Black Muslims, worships Allah and practices some rituals of the orthodox Muslim religion, with certain variations of its own, especially in the sphere of race.

It teaches that original man, when the world was a paradise, was black, and that white man is a degenerate and inferior offshoot, destined to rule the world for 6,000 years and then be destroyed. The 6,000-year period is now ending, and black people can save themselves from the coming catastrophe only by withdrawing, by separating, from the white man and following Muhammad, the Messenger of Allah.

From a scientific standpoint, Black Muslim mythology is no more and no less fantastic or bizarre than other religions. But the Black Muslims are a *movement* as well as a religious group, providing a kind of haven and hope and salvation for outcasts, encouragement at self-reform, brotherhood, and solidarity against a cruel and oppressive world.

I am not going to go into detail about the Black Muslims; you can find plenty about it in writing. The point is that Malcolm experienced a genuine religious conversion in prison, believing that Elijah Muhammad was a holy man, and that the Nation of Islam provided a path of salvation not only for him but for his people.

While in prison this dropout after the eighth grade began to educate himself and learn how to speak and debate, so that he could participate more effectively in the movement after he got out. Not knowing how else to proceed, he started with a dictionary, copying into a tablet words beginning with "A" that might be helpful. He was astonished to find so many "A" words, filling a tablet with them alone. He went through to "Z," and then, he writes, "for the first time, I could pick up a book and actually understand what the book was saying." The story speaks volumes about the quality of education in Michigan—and the U.S.

From then until he left prison, he spent all the time he could in the library, "picking up some more books." Within a few years he was to become the most respected debater in the country, taking on one and all—politicians, college professors, journalists, anyone, black or white, bold enough to meet him.

There are tremendous reservoirs of talent and even genius locked up in the black ghettos and white slums, among the masses—which can be set free and put to work when they acquire hope and purpose.

After six years in prison, when Malcolm was twenty-seven, he won a parole by getting a job with his oldest brother, Wilfred, as a furniture salesman in the Detroit ghetto. That was the spring of 1952. Later that year he traveled to Chicago to hear Elijah Muhammad, and he met him. He was accepted into the movement and given the name of Malcolm X. He volunteered his organizing services in Detroit, and did so well that he was made assistant minister of the Detroit mosque, after the membership had tripled.

At the end of 1953 he went to Chicago to live with Muhammad and be trained by him for some months. Muhammad sent him to Philadelphia, which had no mosque; in less than three months a mosque had been formed. He was obviously a man of unusual talent, energy, and devotion. Muhammad picked him to head the movement in New York, and he went back to Harlem in 1954, before he was thirty years old. In a few short years his work helped to transform the Black Muslims from a virtually unnoticed to a nationally known organization; and he himself had become one of the country's most noted figures, one of the most desired speakers on the nation's campuses, and the object of admiration by the most militant youth.

Before proceeding chronologically, I want to say a few words about Malcolm as a public speaker. I am not an expert in this field and I hope somebody who is will make a study of it. There is certainly plenty of material, thanks to the fact that many of his talks were taped and are readily available.

His speaking style was unique—plain, direct as an arrow, devoid of flowery trimming. He used metaphors and figures of speech that were lean and simple, rooted in the ordinary daily experience of his audiences. He knew what the masses think and how they feel, their strengths and weaknesses. He reached right into their minds and hearts without wasting a word; and he never tried to flatter them. Despite an extraordinary ability to move and arouse his listeners, his main appeal was to reason, not to emotion.

This is true even about speeches where he was presenting ideas that he abandoned in the last year of his life, such as the last great speech he made as a Black Muslim—his speech to the Grass Roots Conference in Detroit in November 1963, which is available from the Afro-American Broadcasting and Recording Company. It is one of his best speeches—although, I repeat, it does not reflect his thinking at the end—and worth listening and relistening to, because of the qualities I have been trying to pinpoint. Because his main appeal was to reason, he was the very opposite of a demagogue, the very opposite of what the kept press called him.

It was also a style very different from Elijah Muhammad's. I don't mean only that Malcolm commanded the weapons of wit and humor, which are alien to Muhammad. Muhammad's appeal was to faith, to authority (divine authority), to the hereafter; Malcolm's appeal was to reason, to logic; it dealt with the real and the present, even when he was expounding Muhammad's line. To be able to listen to Muhammad for any length of time you had to be a believer, convinced in advance, while Malcolm seemed to achieve his greatest success with non-Muslims.

These few remarks about Malcolm as a speaker are admittedly inadequate; I make them only in the hope of interesting someone more qualified than I to study and write about it. I wanted only to convey the idea that there rarely has been a man in America better able to communicate ideas to the most oppressed people; and that this was not just a matter of technique, which can be learned and applied in any situation by almost anybody, but that it was the rare case of a man in closest communion with the oppressed, able to speak to them because he spoke for them, because he identified himself with them, an authentic expression of their yearning for freedom, a true product of their growth in the same way that Lenin was a product of the Russian people.

We come now to the end of the second period of Malcolm's life, 1963, and the split with Muhammad, which was consummated in March 1964. The year 1963 was a year of stirring and movement in the Negro struggle, with hundreds of thousands in the streets; the year that the struggle moved from the South to the Northern ghettos, where the Black Muslims were strongest. It was not yet a revolution, but a prelude to revolutionary struggles. This was the situation that sharpened a dilemma and then produced a crisis in the Black Muslims.

By their militant stance, they had helped to push other Negro organizations to the left. This was their positive contribution. But they were on the sidelines of the struggle, not participants. They talked in angry tones, but did nothing when non-Muslim Negroes were under attack. They were separated not only from whites but from Negro militants.

Among the members, younger and less conservative than in the pre-Malcolm period, signs could be detected of a desire to get into the battle, to pass from propaganda to action. Muhammad tried to allay the ferment; one example was his call, at the organization's national convention in February 1963, for independent black political action. But he soon pulled back from this and other moves that might have drawn the Black Muslims out of their abstentionism. When the Freedom Now Party was started six months later, he refused to endorse it or let the members join.

The occasion for the split was a remark made by Malcolm after John F. Kennedy's death in November 1963, followed by Muhammad's silencing of Malcolm with a virtual suspension that was deliberately intended to be humiliating. But this was only the occasion, not the cause. The basic factor behind the split was the growth of militancy and mass action in the Negro community, and the different ways in which the two main tendencies in the Black Muslims wanted to respond to the masses knocking on the doors of their mosques.

There is an instructive relation between the way Malcolm came into the Black Muslims and the way he left. He turned to them from a state of isolation, not only the physical isolation of prison, but an alienation from society generally and from his own people as well. His years in the Black Muslims had been good for the organization, and they were good for him. He had traveled all over the country as

Muhammad's chief trouble-shooter, and he knew the ghetto nationally as no one else did. His vision had broadened, his interests had widened.

He entered the Black Muslims because he was alone and lost, and he left, you could say, because now he was in closest touch with the Negro people, attuned to their needs and wants more than the Black Muslims were or wanted him to be; because he was becoming the spokesman of a growing multitude looking for a new road; because he had found a new role, or rather because a new role had been thrust upon him, which his whole life's experience told him he had to accept, however difficult it would be.

It could not have been an easy decision. Consider the circumstances: thirty-eight years old; a wife and several dependent children; a secure post, relatively well paid, home provided, car provided, expenses; great prestige; a position in an organization second in authority to a man in his late sixties who was not in good health. Some men in his place would have taken the easy way—keep quiet, do as you are told, stay out of the line of fire, mend your fences, and wait. That's the American way—in business, government, church, fraternal, and labor circles.

But Malcolm was not that kind of man. He had been disturbed to see that Muhammad and some of his ministers were, like other preachers of puritanism, not living in accord with the strict puritanical code they prescribed for the rank-and-file Black Muslims. He tried to overlook things like this—his eyes were mainly turned to the outside world of the broad Negro struggle. He was not the only minister who knew that new, bolder, and more active policies were needed if the Black Muslims were to fulfill their real responsibilities to the Negro people. But the other ministers who recognized the need for change—they played it safe. They weren't Malcolm X.

Malcolm had what can be called a second rebirth early in 1964 when he decided his place was with the Negro masses more than with Muhammad's organization. As a Black Muslim leader, he had rejected corrupt American society. Now he passed from merely rejecting it (a negative, passive position) to rebelling against it and organizing to change it (a positive, active position). That was the essence of the change.

Some ultraleftists in the Negro community did not understand this and talked condescendingly about Malcolm's becoming "weak" or "soft." But the American ruling class and its spokesmen understood what was happening, and they were more hostile to him after the split than before. And they had greater reason to hate and fear him after he set out to build a new movement. That is why, as George Novack puts it, he "was crucified by the paid press long before he was martyred by the assassin's bullets."

We have heard the expression, "the new Malcolm X." It is appropriate in some ways, misleading in others. Some of his ideas did change starting last March, but others did not. Let us at least mention those that did not change before examining those that did:

That Negroes can get their freedom only by fighting for it;

That the government is a racist government and is not going to grant freedom;

That gradualism, the program of the liberals, white and black, is not the road to equality;

That Uncle Toms must be exposed and opposed;

That Negroes must rely on themselves and control their own struggle;

That Negroes must determine their own strategy and tactics;

That Negroes must select their own leaders.

—These are ideas that Malcolm believed before he left the Black Muslims, and that he still believed the day he died.

In approaching the immensely difficult and exhausting job of building a new movement, in opposition to new as well as old enemies— a task which radicals should best be able to understand and sympathize with—Malcolm showed from the start that he did not want merely a replica of the Black Muslim structure plus some modifications in policy. He wanted a different kind of organization, with a different kind of relation between the leaders and ranks.

The Black Muslims built everything around a mystique of leadership, faith in and submission to a divine, all-wise chief. That Malcolm wanted something radically different could be seen from the statement he made at his first press conference after the split. He denied that he was "expert in any particular field." He called for help in the form of ideas and suggestions from all quarters, especially students, white or black.

He not only accepted advice, but sought it. He not only invited criticism, but welcomed it. I am aware of one such case personally. I never met Malcolm or saw him in person, but I wrote many articles about him, most of them supporting and defending him. It was typical of him, I think, that the only one of these articles about which he sent me a message of appreciation was one that was most critical of some implications in a speech he had made.

When he read something useful or pertinent to the problems of his organization, he would go out of his way to get copies for his fellow leaders so that they could read and think about it and develop informed and collective attitudes. On the day he was killed, he was scheduled to present for discussion his ideas on the program of the Organization of Afro-American Unity. It is plain that he was trying to build a far more democratic organization and a far more collective leadership than the Black Muslims ever dreamed of. This is evident also from the fact that he did not fear to associate with radicals and refused to bar them from the organization, despite the discontent of some of the more conservative members.

Malcolm's courage was not only physical, but intellectual. We can appreciate its magnitude only if we fully understand the degree of his dependence on and subordination to Muhammad before the split. For more than twelve years, for most of his adult life, he had been to Muhammad like a son to a father—no, more than that, for few sons are so voluntarily and so long obedient. And then, with very little advance notice, he was on his own. Three days before his death he told a *New York Times* interviewer: "I was the spokesman for the Black Muslims. I believed in Elijah Muhammad more strongly than the Christians do in Jesus. I believed in him so strongly that my mind, my body, my voice functioned 100 percent for him and the movement. My belief led others to believe." In contrast, he continued, "I feel like a man who has been asleep somewhat and under someone else's control. I feel what I'm thinking and saying now is for myself. Before, it was for and by the guidance of Elijah Muhammad. Now I think with my own mind, sir."

To think with his own mind—that is what all the forces at the command of the ruling class in this country are organized to discourage and prevent the Negro from doing. You need intellectual as well as physical courage to think and say things for yourself, to think new thoughts, to search out ideas that have been forbidden by the ruling class, to seek them among the Mau Mau in Kenya, or the Simbas in the Congo. That is the true mark of an open, honest, and free mind—and of a revolutionary leader.

Malcolm remained a believer in Islam after the split with Muhammad, but it was in the official and orthodox Islam he saw during his trip to Mecca last year. He praised Muhammad even as he left his organization, thinking or hoping that friction with the Black Muslims could be avoided while he turned his attention to the broad Negro struggle. With the advantage of hindsight, we can see this hope was unfounded. An independent movement of the Malcolm X type was a threat to *every* vested interest in the country, *every* privileged hierarchy. And it did not take long for Muhammad to launch ruthless and slanderous attacks designed to isolate Malcolm, because he feared that otherwise he would be deserted by his own members. Perhaps Malcolm might still be alive if he had realized from the start how much he imperiled the status quo, and had acted and prepared differently. This we don't know, can't know.

Malcolm believed in black unity after as well as before the split. But as a Black Muslim, what he meant and had to mean was black unity under the leadership and control of Muhammad, and with unquestioning acceptance of his religious dogmas and discipline. The kind of black unity Malcolm sought after the split was the unity of all Negroes, whatever their religions, whatever their philosophies, so long as they were ready to fight for freedom.

It was a movement away from religious sectarianism toward non-sectarian mass action. But this aim could not be fulfilled by his first organizational step at the time of the split—the founding of the Muslim Mosque, Incorporated. As a religious organization, it would obviously be limited in its appeal. Malcolm soon corrected this by forming the broad Organization of Afro-American Unity. The selection of a religious group first showed how closely he was tied to his past even one year ago; the addition of the OAAU not many weeks later showed how rapidly he was able to transcend the limitations carried over from his past.

We must spend some time on the issue of self-defense, or, as the press called it, "violence." We have to spend it, although the truth is so obvious, because the press centered their attacks around this issue.

Malcolm always was for self-defense—in his teens, when he was part of the underworld; when he was a Black Muslim; and in his last year. In each of these three periods, however, the idea had a different content for him. The Black Muslims say you have the right to defend yourself when attacked, and that this right is granted by Allah and his messenger. Malcolm validated the right on political and constitutional grounds; he brought it down from heaven to earth. The Black Muslims defend themselves, but Malcolm went further and said all Negroes should defend themselves; with him the right became specific, concrete, and practical. The difference was apparent when Muhammad's first attack on Malcolm revolved around Malcolm's advocacy of defensive rifle clubs.

Seeing many students in the audience, I shall try to convey my point this way. Let me suggest that one or several of you prepare a research paper on the subject: "How the Press Reported Malcolm X's Views on Violence." It would be very enlightening. It would give you insight, through one example, of the way 99 percent of the American people get the "information" on the basis of which they form their ideas. It would illuminate more than the single example; it would reveal some basic features of American society as a whole and how it is controlled through propaganda posing as news or fact.

As a model for such a research paper on Malcolm and violence, I recommend a recent book called *A Curtain of Ignorance* by Felix Greene, a journalist familiar with China. What it does is compare the facts about China with what the American press has been writing about China for the past fifteen years. The result is devastating. I will read but one example.

In 1963 Mao Tse-tung issued, at the suggestion of Robert F. Williams, a statement on racial discrimination in the U.S. The key sentence said: "I call upon the workers, peasants, revolutionary intellectuals, enlightened elements of the bourgeoisie, and other enlightened persons of all colors—white, black, yellow, brown, etc.—to unite to oppose racial discrimination practiced by U.S. imperialism and to support the American Negroes in their struggle against racial discrimination."

Here is how the *Christian Century* (and many other publications in this country) described that statement: "A summons to colored peoples to unite in war against the white race was issued from Peking in the name of Mao Tse-tung. His call for worldwide racial war reflects a degree of hate and desperation which can only be described as psychotic."

The writer of my proposed research paper will find Greene's book useful because *exactly* the same method was used with Malcolm's statements on violence. And its use was no more accidental in one case than in the other.

Those of you who heard Malcolm know that he did not advocate violence; he advocated that Negroes defend themselves when attacked. He said it a hundred times, he said it a thousand times. He said that he was opposed to violence and wanted to stop it, and that Negroes could contribute to stopping it by letting the attackers know they would defend themselves. He could have said it a million times and the readers of the American press still would not have known the truth.

Take the *New York Times*. This is supposed to be the best daily paper in the country, in the world. Urbane, sophisticated, liberal on certain civil liberties and civil rights questions. But it hated Malcolm with a fury I cannot recollect it showing to anyone else in the thirty years I have been reading it. The mask slipped the day Malcolm was killed, and the ugly face of American capitalism showed through in the editorial that appeared the next morning. There is a Latin saying: *Speak nothing but good about the dead.* The *Times*'s approach to Malcolm was: *Speak nothing good about the dead, and if you must, twist it to make it look bad.*

"He was a case history, as well as an extraordinary and twisted man, turning many true gifts to evil purpose," says the *Times* editorial. ("Case history" and "twisted" is their way of saying Malcolm was mentally unbalanced. So he was insane, and evil to boot.)

". . . his ruthless and fanatical belief in violence . . . marked him for fame, and for a violent end." (So his alleged belief is linked to his death, in some kind of cause-and-effect relation; he was responsible for his own murder.)

". . . . he did not seek to fit into society or into the life of his own people. . . . The world he saw through those horn-rimmed glasses of his was distorted and dark. But he made it darker still with his exaltation of fanaticism. Yesterday someone came out of that darkness that he spawned and killed him." (The darkness that *he* spawned! So Malcolm was not only mad and evil, he also possessed magical power—he made himself look like 39, but he must have been at least 350 years old to have "spawned" racial violence.) The editorial concludes with the magnanimous concession that the murder "demands an investigation." Not because it was a criminal act, but because it "could easily touch off a war of vengeance of the kind he himself fomented."

Now why is this? Suppose that I, a so-called white man, or any white person, went downtown and stood on a box and said, "White people should defend themselves *when attacked.*" Would I be branded an advocate of violence, a racist, or a fanatic? No, the worst I would be called would be a nut.

And if a white person got up there after me and said, "White people should defend their interests when they are attacked in Cuba or Vietnam by sending invasion armies or bombers," would the press condemn him as a fomentor of violence, or a racist fanatic? No, some would say, "Of course, it goes without saying," and others would declare, "That man belongs in the White House." The White House, not the nuthouse.

What is the difference? The difference is that black people, not whites, are being attacked or are subject to attack. And the very thought of someone encouraging Negroes to defend themselves makes the apologists for American racism see red, or black. So much so that they can hardly work up the pretense that they are in any way unhappy about Malcolm's murder. This difference shows beyond doubt how permeated with racism this country and its press are. The only other country in the world with such phobias and psychoses is South Africa.

It is too bad that so much time has to be spent explaining such obvious truths, because Malcolm's stand on this issue was not the central part of his philosophy—just the most controversial. It was an indispensable part of his program, for how can anyone expect to win freedom unless he is willing to defend his person, rights, and property against violence designed to terrorize and silence him? But it was not a central part, and is not, by itself, the solution to the Negro's problems. Even when Negroes organize for self-defense, as they should and inevitably will, they will still not be free, because inequality is built into this society, in every warp and woof; the system itself exudes and perpetuates inequality.

Next is the question of race. Here Malcolm made a very pronounced change in his thinking. Partly through the influence of Islam, a religion which views and treats all races alike, and partly through his contact with revolutionaries in many countries, he threw overboard the whole Black Muslim mythology about superior and inferior races and its doctrine about inherent evil and degeneracy in a white skin.

Repudiating racism in all forms, he resolved to judge men and movements on the basis of their deeds, not their color or race. Deeds, not words; and he was pretty shrewd about distinguishing between the two, as in the case of white liberals (or black liberals, for that matter). He developed an historical approach to racism. He knew American whites had been conditioned, miseducated, and infected on race worse than most European whites, for example, and he remained more on guard with Americans. He distinguished in a similar way between the older and younger white generations in America.

When Young Socialist Alliance leaders interviewed him and asked what he considered to be the cause of race prejudice, he didn't give anything resembling the Black Muslim position. "Ignorance and greed," he replied. A scientific socialist of any race might turn the three words around, saying "Greed and ignorance," and might expand on the theme at greater length, but would not say anything essentially different. "You can't have capitalism without racism," he said on an earlier occasion.

Malcolm had been abroad before his break with Muhammad, but only briefly, carrying out assignments for Muhammad, not on his own. But after the break in 1964 he traveled to and through Africa and the Mideast twice, spending almost half of his remaining life abroad—studying, searching, discussing, learning, seeking help and giving it. And when he returned he was not just a sympathizer of the colonial revolution, but a staunch internationalist, on the side of the oppressed and exploited masses of the world against their oppressors and exploiters—whose central fountainhead he recognized to be U.S. imperialism, the dominant force in what he called the international power structure. No one in the world denounced the U.S. role in the Congo more forcefully and effectively.

One purpose of his trips was of course to mobilize African support behind the project to put the U.S. government on trial in the United Nations for the continued oppression of American Negroes, with which he had limited success. But the State Department credited him, or rather blamed him, for a good part of the strong stand against U.S. imperialism taken by African nations in the United Nations at the time of the latest atrocities in the Congo. As he knew, the CIA and similar agencies take an interest in what the State Department doesn't like.

Those who heard him in Detroit the week before his murder knew about his hope to unite the many millions of the oppressed in Latin America and the Caribbean together with their Afro-American brothers and sisters against their common exploiter.

So he was simultaneously broadening his horizons and zeroing in on American imperialism—this product of the segregated, locked-in ghetto who broke through and over the walls of national boundary and race to become an internationalist; this internationalist who admired John Killens's definition of a patriot: "Dignity was his country, Manhood was his government, and Freedom was his land."

In the area of political action Malcolm was also far ahead of the Black Muslims. That didn't take much doing, since they abstain from politics. He favored Negroes' organizing politically and running and electing their own candidates, and driving out of office black stooges of the major parties. He participated in a Harlem conference on independent political action two months before his death.

But his position on politics was largely general. He said he found some good in what the Freedom Now Party was doing, and while he was in Africa last summer he briefly gave consideration to an offer that he run on the Michigan FNP ticket for the U.S. Senate; he decided instead to remain in Africa longer. However, he never affiliated with the FNP, for reasons not discussed publicly; maybe he thought the FNP was premature or launched without sufficient groundwork on too narrow a basis.

While his thinking on politics was still in a process of development, and uncompleted, there was nothing general or tentative about his attitude to the capitalist parties and the two-party system. To him they were both enemies of the Negro people, currently as well as historically, and neither merited an iota of support from Negroes. He had nothing but contempt for the Communist Party's support of Johnson in 1964.

While he did not endorse Clifton DeBerry, the Socialist Workers Party candidate for president, he did attack both of DeBerry's major opponents; and in his own way made it easier for DeBerry to get a hearing from Harlem audiences, thus indicating a measure of sympathy. He said he would be willing under certain conditions to consider running as an independent candidate for mayor of New York against the Democratic and Republican candidates in 1965. In terms of the political spectrum he stood on the radical side, although he had not reached strong conclusions about *how* to organize independent black political power.

The speech Malcolm had started to make when he was shot down was to deal with the program of the Organization of Afro-American Unity, and of the militant black movement generally. We know that he had been thinking about the question of "alliances," the question of the independent Negro movement's relations with other forces in this country, and that he had circulated among other OAAU leaders literature dealing with some aspects of this subject.

Even if we did not know that, it would be logical to assume that he would touch on this question, because no organization defines itself and clarifies its own program and perspectives without simultaneously defining its relations to its enemies and its friends, present or potential. Now we may never know where his thinking had led him on this point, and can only speculate. But even speculation can be oriented by some definite facts.

At his first press conference last March, Malcolm had this to say on the question of alliances: "Whites can help us, but they can't join us. There can be no black-white unity until there is first some black unity. There can be no workers' solidarity until there is first some racial solidarity. We cannot think of uniting with others, until we have first united among ourselves."

This, as I pointed out at that time, is not the statement of a man claiming that black and white working-class solidarity is unnecessary, or that it is impossible. On the contrary, it is the statement of a man explaining one of the conditions through which workers' solidarity may be achieved on a broad and durable basis. And if I may quote myself for one more sentence, I noted: "Revolutionary socialists will certainly agree [with Malcolm] that a meaningful and mutually beneficial labor-Negro alliance will not be forged until the Negro people are organized independently and strongly enough, numerically and ideologically, to assure that their interests cannot be subordinated or sold out by the other partner or partners in any alliance."

The subject must have come up often during his subsequent travels abroad, where his ideas were strongly influenced during his last year. But he stuck to his position. When he spoke at a Militant Labor Forum in New York last May, he said: "In my recent travels into the African countries and others, it was impressed upon me the importance of having a working unity among all peoples, black as well as white. But the only way this is going to be brought about is the Negroes have to be in unity first."

So far as I have been able to learn, that remained Malcolm's position to the end. He was not opposed to alliances with other forces, including labor, provided they were the right kinds of alliances and provided the Negro part of the alliance was independently organized, so that it could guard against betrayal by being able to pull out of any alliance that went bad.

There is no doubt whatever in my mind that Malcolm would have favored an independent mass black movement making alliances with a radicalized mass labor movement when conditions produced two such components for an alliance. I have no doubt about it because he was willing, even now, in the absence of two such mass movements, to collaborate with radical whites under certain conditions. A man willing to collaborate with numerically weak radical forces, as I will try to show Malcolm was, would have to be out of his mind not to collaborate with mass radical forces.

And whatever the *New York Times* and *Muhammad Speaks* say, Malcolm was not out of his mind.

Next let us consider briefly Malcolm's attitudes to capitalism and socialism. In an interview with the *Young Socialist** he stated: "It is impossible for capitalism to survive, primarily because the system of capitalism needs some blood to suck. Capitalism used to be like an eagle, but now it's more like a vulture . . . and can only suck the blood of the helpless. As the nations of the world free themselves, then capitalism has less and less victims, less to suck, and it becomes weaker and weaker. It's only a matter of time in my opinion before it will collapse completely." Marxists might question whether capitalism will collapse, or have to be collapsed, but who can question that in his last months Malcolm was taking an unequivocally anticapitalist position?

Malcolm did not learn about socialism by reading Marx, but he managed to learn about it anyway. He learned about it from the colonial revolution, especially its prosocialist contingent. He had discussions with Castro and Che Guevara and Algerian socialists and socialists in Ghana, Guinea, Zanzibar, and elsewhere, including the United States. When he was asked last May at the Militant Labor Forum what kind of political system he wanted, he said: "I don't know. But I'm flexible. As was stated earlier, all of the countries that are emerging today from under the shackles of colonialism are turning towards socialism. I don't think it's an accident. Most of the countries that were colonial powers were capitalist countries and the last bulwark of capitalism today is America and it's impossible for a white person today to believe in capitalism and not believe in racism. You can't have capitalism without racism. And if you find a person without racism and you happen to get that person into conversation and they have a philosophy that makes

---

* This interview, held on January 18, 1965, and published in the *Young Socialist*, March–April 1965, has been reprinted in *By Any Means Necessary* (Pathfinder Press, 1970)—Ed.

you sure they don't have this racism in their outlook, usually they're socialists or their political philosophy is socialism." Clifton DeBerry was sitting on the same platform, and took the floor to comment on when and where flexibility was correct: in tactics, yes, but not in relation to the principle that the capitalist system and capitalist parties are enemies of freedom, justice, and equality. To which Malcolm replied: "And that's the most intelligent answer I've ever heard on that question." So I think it fair to say that the legacy of Malcolm is not only plainly anticapitalist but also prosocialist. I do not say he was a Marxist—he wasn't—and we can only guess if in his further evolution he would have become one, as Castro did in his later development. But that clearly can be reckoned as a possibility.

A few words about Malcolm's relations with the revolutionary socialists, the Socialist Workers Party and the Young Socialist Alliance: The record is plain about our attitude to Malcolm. We regarded him as one of the most gifted and important leaders of the struggle while he was still a Black Muslim. When he started his own movement, we called it a momentous development that might turn the struggle onto the road to victory, and publicly pledged our aid in the job he was undertaking. For this we got abuse and condemnation from so-called radicals and liberals; our white members were called "white black nationalists" and other names because we supported Malcolm's movement. All this was long before he had said a single word favorable to socialism, and when the image of him in most so-called radical minds was of a man who would rather die than have anything to do with whites, even revolutionary whites.

On the other side was Malcolm's attitude to us. As a Black Muslim he used to buy the *Militant* when it was sold outside his rallies. He later said that even then he urged Negroes to read it. Less than a month after his break with Muhammad, he spoke at the Militant Labor Forum in New York, and publicly praised the *Militant* for telling the truth and wished it success. He spoke for the Militant Labor Forum another two times during the next nine months, after each of his trips abroad. He wasn't even scheduled to speak the second time: his secretary, James Shabazz, was to be part of a panel, but Malcolm phoned and asked if he would be acceptable in James Shabazz's place; and of course he was.

At most of the OAAU rallies he would put in a plug for the *Militant*, without any solicitation on our part. He smoothed the way for it to be sold at Harlem stands and shops. In January, when he gave his interview to the *Young Socialist*, he discussed with the YSA leaders the probability of his making a tour of the nation's campuses in collaboration with the YSA later this year. He would almost surely have spoken here at Debs Hall for the Friday Night Socialist Forum while making that tour. Black SWP and YSA members were welcome to join his organization; whites associated with the *Militant* were welcome to attend OAAU rallies.

So our relations were friendly and mutually helpful—on our part, because we believed that he and we were on the same side in the struggle, had the same enemies, and were traveling in the same direction. In our 1963 convention resolution, the Socialist Workers Party had stated that black nationalism and revolutionary socialism "are not only compatible but complementary forces, that should be welded closely together in thought and action." We predicted that would happen, and so far as Malcolm and we were concerned, it was beginning to happen.

On his part, I think, collaboration was taking place because he felt that we, unlike the liberals, unlike the Communist Party, unlike the Socialist Party, unlike most white radicals, did not want to subordinate his movement or the Negro struggle generally to the government, to the Democratic Party, to the American labor bureaucrats, to the privileged bureaucrats in noncapitalist countries, or to anyone else; and that we did and do want the Negro movement to attain full independence of program and action and to develop uninterruptedly in an uncompromisingly militant direction along the lines that best suit its needs.

Once Malcolm was convinced of that, and of our sincerity, as evidenced by our readiness to stick by our principles, however unpopular they might be, there was no bar to our collaboration. I want to stress that he would have taken this attitude to any militant group, even nonsocialist, provided it was, in its own way, independent of the government and opposed to racism.

Let us now conclude this discussion of Malcolm's ideas during the last year of his life by examining his positions on black nationalism and separatism. This is important because some political opponents of Malcolm already are circulating distorted stories about him, alleging that he was on the verge of quitting his movement, going over to his opponents, etc. And important also because there may be some ambiguity about his relation to black nationalism as a result of a statement in his interview in the current issue of the *Young Socialist.*

    Black nationalism and separatism are not the same thing, though unfortunately they are often confused. Separatism is a tendency favoring the withdrawal of Negroes into a separate black nation, either in America or in Africa. Black nationalism is a tendency for Negroes to unite as a group, as a people, in organizations that are Negro-led and Negro-controlled, and sometimes all-black, in order to fight for their freedom. Black nationalism, as it now exists, does not imply any position on the question of a separate nation in the future, for or against. So you can be a black nationalist without being a separatist, although all separatists are black nationalists. You will find a much better and longer analysis of this greatly misunderstood distinction in the Socialist Workers Party's 1963 convention resolution, *Freedom Now: The New Stage in the Struggle for Negro Emancipation* (distributed by Pathfinder Press).

    When Malcolm was a Black Muslim, he was of course a separatist. At his first press conference after leaving the Black Muslims last March, he said he was out to build a black nationalist movement, and the major stress was on black nationalism. But he also had a few words to say about separatism. He said he still thought separation was "the best solution"; previously he would have said the *only* solution. "But," he continued, "separation back to Africa is still a long-range program, and while it is yet to materialize, 22 million of our people who are still here in America need better food, clothing, housing, education, and jobs *right now*" (his emphasis).

At the time I took this to be a declaration of his intention to build a black nationalist movement that would attempt to unite the Negro people in a fight for immediate needs, while at the same time continuing to hold up separation as a nation as an ultimate objective, and to make propaganda for it accordingly. But I was obviously wrong, because after that statement last March I cannot find any place where Malcolm advocated a separate nation. And on May 21, a few hours after returning from his first trip to Africa, when he was asked at a press conference if he thought Negroes should return to Africa, he said he thought they should stay and fight in the United States for what is rightfully theirs.

Perhaps he thought a separate nation, while desirable, was so far off there was no use talking about it. Perhaps he thought it was a divisive issue impeding black unity. Or perhaps he no longer thought it desirable. In any case, he stopped being a separatist at the time of his break with the Black Muslims, or soon after.

What about his position on black nationalism? Everyone called him a nationalist, friend and foe, and there was no question about it until a few weeks ago. Then he was asked, in the *Young Socialist* interview, "How do you define black nationalism, with which you have been identified?"

He began his answer by saying, "I used to define black nationalism as the idea that the black man should control the economy of his community, the politics of his community, and so forth." That is, he used to define it in the traditional way, as I tried to do a few minutes ago.

The second paragraph of Malcolm's reply, which you can read for yourselves in the *Young Socialist,* relates a discussion he had with a white Algerian revolutionary he met in Ghana last May who sought to convince Malcolm that his self-designation as a black nationalist tended to alienate people "who were true revolutionaries dedicated to overturning the system of exploitation that exists on this earth by any means necessary." His third and final paragraph was: "So, I had to do a lot of thinking and reappraising of my definition of black nationalism. Can we sum up the solution to the problems confronting our people as black nationalism? And if you notice, I haven't been using the expression for several months. But I still would be hard pressed to give a specific definition of the overall philosophy which I think is necessary for the liberation of the black people in this country."

Please notice: He was reappraising his *definition* of black nationalism and wondering if it can be *summed up* as the solution; he had stopped using the term, but he had not yet been able to find another definition for the philosophy necessary for black liberation. Now let me offer what I think is the explanation for all this.

Malcolm had been a black nationalist—it was the starting point for all his thinking, the source of his strength and dynamism. And he remained a black nationalist to his last hour, however uncertain he was about what to *call* himself or the program he was trying to formulate. It would be a bad mistake to mix up what he was with what he thought might be a better name for what he was.

The most urgent need of the Negro people is still the mobilization and unification of the Negro masses into an independent movement to fight for their freedom. Black nationalism is still highly progressive because it contributes to that process and to the creation of that kind of movement. But black nationalism is a means, not the end; it is a means, but not the only means; it is probably an indispensable means toward the solution, but it is not the whole solution. It helps to build an independent movement, but it does not necessarily provide the program that will lead such a movement to victory.

In a series of articles in the *Militant* last year, I tried to clarify some questions about black nationalism by noting that there are at least two types of black nationalist. One is the pure-and-simple black nationalist. He is concerned exclusively or primarily with the internal problems of the Negro community, with organizing it, helping it to control the economy of the community, the politics of the community, etc. He is not so concerned with the problems of the total American society, or with the nature of the total society within which the Negro community exists. He has no theory or program for changing that society; for him that's the white man's problem.

Now Malcolm was not that kind of black nationalist, or if he was a year ago, he did not remain that. As he discussed with people in Africa, in the Near East, at the United Nations, and in the United States, as he studied and thought and learned, he began to become a black nationalist plus. Plus what? I have already given you many quotations from his speeches and interviews showing that as he studied the economy, the nature of the political and social system of American capitalism, as he developed greater and keener understanding of how this system functions and how the ruling class rules and how racism is a component and instrument of that rule, he came more and more to the conclusion that not only must the Negro control his own community, but radical changes have to be made in the society as a whole if the Negroes are to achieve their freedom.

Black nationalism, yes. But the solution cannot be *summed up* as only black nationalism. Needed is black nationalism plus fundamental social change; black nationalism plus the transformation of the entire society. Whatever difficulty Malcolm may have had in finding the right name, what he was becoming was black nationalist plus revolutionist. (The *Young Socialist* interview shows that he had great respect for that word.)

There are really only three ways in which it is possible to think of the Negro people getting freedom and equality. One way (notice I said to *think* about getting freedom) is through gradualism; peaceful reform; a little bit now and a little bit more ten years from now. Not Freedom Now, but Freedom Later, which for purposes of Negroes now alive, means Freedom Never. This is the program of Lyndon Johnson, Reuther, King, Wilkins, and Rustin. Malcolm, as we know, flatly rejected this approach.

The second way is through separation, through migration to Africa, or through obtaining part of what is now the United States. Malcolm, as I indicated, had turned away from this approach, what-

ever his reasons may have been for doing so.

The third way—and I repeat there are only these three ways, there are no others—is through the revolutionary reorganization of society, by basically changing the economy, political structure, laws, and educational system, and by replacing the present capitalist ruling class with a new government instituted by the forces that are opposed to racism and determined to uproot it.

From the quotations I read you before on what Malcolm was saying about capitalism and socialism and racism, it is clear that Malcolm tended to favor this third approach, or at least had his eyes turned in that direction. He wasn't sure *if* it could be done, and he wasn't sure *how* it could be done, but he was thinking about it and how it fitted into the program and activity of the Organization of Afro-American Unity.

This, I believe, correctly explains his uncertainty about what to call himself. He was a black nationalist plus, a black nationalist plus a social revolutionist, or in the process of becoming one.

Socialists should be the last to be surprised at such a development. We have for some time been stressing the tendency of nationalism to grow over into and become merged with socialism; we have seen just that transformation occur in Cuba with Castro and his movement, which began as nationalist. We have argued against many opponents that the logical outcome of black nationalism in a country like ours is to reach the most advanced, most radical social and political conclusions. That is why we have advocated and predicted that black nationalists and revolutionary socialists can, should, and will find ways of working together.

Malcolm's uncertainty about the right name arises from the fact that he was doing something new—he was on the road to a synthesis of black nationalism and socialism that would be fitting for the American scene and acceptable to the masses in the black ghetto. He did not complete the synthesis before he was murdered. It remains for others to complete what he was beginning.

Now he is dead, taken from us in what might have been the most important and fruitful year of his life.

Let us not deceive ourselves. It was a stunning blow, as Frank Lovell said at last week's memorial meeting of the Afro-American Broadcasting Company, it was a stunning blow to the Negro people and to those white Americans who want to eradicate the system that breeds racism. Men like Malcolm do not appear often, or in great numbers. The enemies of human progress benefit from his death. The fighters for human progress are weakened and hurt by it.

But a stunning blow to the struggle does not destroy the struggle. Malcolm will not easily be replaced. But he will be replaced. The capitalist system breeds not only racism, but rebels against racism, especially among the youth. Malcolm cannot be replaced overnight, but meanwhile we all can and should strive harder, work harder, fight harder, unite more closely to try to fill the gap left by the death of this man we loved, and give help and encouragement to those destined to replace him.

2

Unanswered questions

by George Breitman

These three articles analyzing the New York daily newspapers' coverage of the assassination of Malcolm X were written in July and August 1965 and were first printed in the Militant, July 12, August 9, and August 23, 1965. When they were reprinted in 1969 as part of a pamphlet entitled The Assassination of Malcolm X, they were introduced by a note in which Breitman said: "The questions I asked about the role of the police in the assassination of Malcolm X were transmitted to the defense attorneys [in the 1966 trial of the three men charged with the assassination] in the hope that they would raise them during the trial. As Herman Porter's reports [on the trial, reprinted in chapter 3 of this book] indicate, they deliberately avoided doing so. Readers should also understand that if the New York police were involved in the assassination (and nothing said or done at the trial, or in the four years since the crime, has absolved them of this charge), that involvement could not have been on their own initiative, but must have resulted from the decision and direction of the government in Washington, that is, the CIA."

THE MISSING 'SECOND' MAN

Some mystifying questions about the assassination of Malcolm X arise if you carefully read the New York newspaper reports printed right after the assassination, as I have just done. Some of them concern the role of the police.

I should explain, at the beginning, that I have no fixed theory about the killing. I don't know if agents of the Black Muslims did it; or if agents of white racists did it; or if agents of the government or the police did it; or if agents of a combination of these forces, who all hated Malcolm, did it. I am, at this point, only asking some questions provoked by studying different editions of the six New York daily papers after the killing.

Certain things seem agreed upon by everybody: The Organization of Afro-American Unity had scheduled a rally on Sunday afternoon, February 21, at the Audubon Ballroom in Harlem. This was one week after Malcolm's home was fire-bombed and he and his family narrowly escaped injury or death. People entering the rally were not searched. On the other hand, they were all scrutinized by OAAU aides as they entered the hall.

Malcolm had just begun to speak when two men began a scuffle deliberately designed to distract the attention of Malcolm's guards. Three men rushed toward Malcolm, opening fire and wounding him mortally; they then ran out of the ballroom, pursued by several of Malcolm's supporters.

Police said that one of the three, identified later as Talmadge Hayer, twenty-two, of Paterson, New Jersey, had received a bullet in the leg by the time he got to the exit of the building. The police also alleged that he had been wounded by Reuben Francis, a Malcolm guard. Hayer was seized outside the building by the people pursuing him. So was another man. The people began to beat and kick Hayer and the second man. Police arrived and rescued the two being beaten, taking them away from the crowd. The third man got away. He got away because the crowd did not catch him. Hayer and the second man also would have got away if the crowd hadn't caught and held them until the police showed up.

Now let us turn to the *New York Herald Tribune* dated Monday, February 22. This is a morning paper, which means that the first edition of the paper dated Monday actually appeared Sunday evening, a few hours after the killing. The top headline in the first (city) edition reads: "Malcolm X Slain by Gunmen as 400 in Ballroom Watch." The subhead, over the lead article by Jimmy Breslin, reads: "Police Rescue Two Suspects."

Breslin's story in this edition reports that Hayer was "taken to Bellevue Prison Ward and was sealed off by a dozen policemen. The other suspect was taken to the Wadsworth Avenue precinct, where the city's top policemen immediately converged and began one of the heaviest homicide investigations this city has ever seen."

Next we turn to a later (late city) edition of the same paper for the same day. The top headline is unchanged. But the subhead is different. This time it reads, "Police Rescue One Suspect." The "second" suspect has dropped not only out of the headline, but out of Breslin's story too. Nothing about his being caught and beaten by the crowd, nothing about his being rescued by the police, nothing about his being taken to the Wadsworth station, nothing about the city's top police converging on that station. Not only does he disappear from Breslin's story in the late city edition, but he disappears from the *Herald Tribune* altogether from that date to this.

Perhaps the whole thing never happened? Perhaps Breslin, in the heat of the moment, had in his first story reported a mere rumor as a fact, and, being unable to verify it, decided not to repeat it in later editions?

But there are three morning papers in New York, and in their first editions they *all* said it happened. For example, let us examine the first (city) edition of the *New York Times* for February 22. The subhead is very clear: "Police Hold Two for Questioning." From the *Times*'s city edition, we even learn the name of the cop who captured the "second" man. It is Patrolman Thomas Hoy, who is quoted as saying he had "grabbed a suspect" being chased by some people.

But when we turn to the late city edition of the same *Times*, printed only a few hours later, we find that its subhead, too, has changed. It now reads: "One Is Held in Killing." But the story hasn't yet been changed altogether. Patrolman Hoy still remains in the story, and so does the "second" man who has dropped out of the subhead. In fact, the story has more about Hoy than it had in the city edition.

This time the *Times* reports: "'As I brought him to the front of the ballroom, the crowd began beating me and the suspect,' Patrolman Hoy said. He said he put this man—not otherwise identified later for newsmen—into a police car to be taken to the Wadsworth Avenue station." Then Hoy's captive disappears from the *Times* as completely and as permanently as he did from the *Herald Tribune,* and from all the other daily papers. But there cannot be any doubt in the mind of anyone reading the accounts I have cited that a second man was captured and taken away by the police.

Who was he?

Why did the press lose interest in him so suddenly, at a time that it was filling its pages with all kinds of material about the murder, including the silliest trivialities and wildest rumors? Was it because the police "advised" them to?

Why did Patrolman Hoy deem the "second" man to be a suspect? What was he doing at the time Hoy grabbed him? Why did the crowd deem him to be a suspect? What had they seen him doing before Hoy grabbed him?

Why did the city's "top policemen" surround him with a wall of silence that has not been pierced for four and a half months? If they decided he was innocent, why didn't they say so publicly? That is the usual practice. Why didn't they at least announce his name? That is also usually done. What did the "second" man know about the murder plot and the identity of the killers?

It is extremely difficult to figure out why the police (and the press) behaved in this way. It leads to another question: Could the "second" man have been a police agent? Fantastic? Only if you don't know anything about the police, FBI, CIA, etc.

It is standard procedure for them to infiltrate radical, black nationalist, and just militant organizations. Sometimes, as the recent "Statue of Liberty"* case showed, these police agents worm their

---

* In 1965 three Black activists and a Quebecois were arrested on charges of conspiring to blow up the Statue of Liberty, the Washington Monument, and the

NEW YORK

Herald  Tribune

THE CITY

Established 124 Years Ago. A European Edition Is Published Daily in Paris

MONDAY, FEBRUARY 22, 1965

TEN CENTS

Malcolm X Slain by Gunmen
As 400 in Ballroom Watch

The Feud That Led To Death

By Robert W. White

A long-brewing feud between Elijah Muhammad, spiritual leader of the Black Muslims, and his heir-apparent, Malcolm X, boiled over 14 months ago when Malcolm X stood on a platform in New York and shouted his exultation over the assassination of President John F. Kennedy.

"Chickens coming home to roost never did make me sad; they've always made me glad," he shouted from the stage of Manhattan Center.

SHOCK

Elijah Muhammad, declaring the Black Muslims were shocked "with the rest of the world" at the assassination, promptly imposed complete silence on the man who had been his principal spokesman. Ninety days later, on March 8, 1964, Malcolm X announced his departure from the ranks of the Black Muslims to organize a Black Nationalist movement of his own.

Yesterday, the chickens did, indeed, come home to roost. Police declared the assassination of Malcolm X to be the "result of a long-standing feud between the followers of Elijah Muhammad and the

Chickens coming home to roost never did make me sad; they've always made me glad!

—Malcolm X exulting at the assassination of President Kennedy

Police Rescue Two Suspects

By Jimmy Breslin

© 1965 New York Herald Tribune, Inc.

Up in front of the ballroom, on the stage, somebody was saying, "Malcolm is a man who would give his life for you."

Then the people, 400 of them, the best crowd Malcolm X had drawn in three years, sat up from their wooden folding chairs and clapped for 45 seconds while Malcolm X came up to the rostrum and stood there, waiting to talk.

The rostrum came up to Malcolm's chest. But it was made out of thin wood and the bullets would go through it easy. The applause stopped and the people began to sit down and everybody was looking at Malcolm X and only the two guys in the back of the ballroom made their move.

They came right down the aisle, reaching for the guns in their pockets, and somebody began to yell and Malcolm, who didn't hear it, was saying, "Ladies and Gentlemen" when the two started shooting.

They shot right through the rostrum. They fired about 16 shots and the bullets went through the thin wood and Malcolm took at least three of them in his body. Everybody in the room, this good crowd of 400 that he had drawn, was screaming and tumbling to the floor and Malcolm X stood at the rostrum and then he tilted over and went down, the side of his head slamming on the wooden floor. He lay on the stage and began to die.

ON THE STREET

The two who shot him headed out a door on the side of the stage which took them down two flights of stairs to the street. But a big bodyguard, screaming, was after them and more of Malcolm's men spilled onto the stairs. They caught up with the two gunmen out on the street and were trying to kill them when the police rumbled on top of definitely the popped it.

But they had done what they were supposed to do. They had come to the Audubon Auditorium, an old, wooden-floored dance hall on 166th Street and Broadway, and they

NEW YORK

Herald Tribune

THE LATE CITY

Established 124 Years Ago. A European Edition is Published Daily in Paris

MONDAY, FEBRUARY 22, 1965

TEN CENTS

Chickens coming home to roost never did make me sad; they've always made me glad!

—Malcolm X exulting at the assassination of President Kennedy

Malcolm X Slain by Gunmen
As 400 in Ballroom Watch

The Feud That Led To Death

Police Rescue One Suspect

The case of the missing suspect. Press at first reported two men arrested, later changed their stories with no explanation.

way into positions where they can carry out provocations or cause other damage, in addition to merely "reporting" what happens inside the organizations infiltrated.

We do not have to speculate about whether or not the police infiltrated the Organization of Afro-American Unity and whether or not such police agents were present at the Audubon Ballroom at the time of the assassination. The answer is yes, without any speculation. A "high police official" said, as reported in the *Herald Tribune* February 23, that "several" members of the highly secretive Bureau of Special Services (BOSS) were present in the audience at the time of the killing.

After talking to this high police official, *Herald Tribune* staff member Milton Lewis wrote: "It is no secret that BOSS police—who never wear uniforms—have credentials to cover almost any situation, so that if they were required to have a card or emblem of the Black Nationalist sect it is a safe bet that they had them."

So perhaps the "second" man was a police agent, and perhaps the strange behavior of the top police results from their desire to protect one of their own "several" men present at the Audubon. But in that case, the question must be asked again, and such questions will keep on being asked until the whole story is told: Why was the crowd convinced that the "second" man was one of the killers?

THE ROLE OF THE POLICE

"Why don't you admit that the Black Muslims killed Malcolm X, instead of trying to cast suspicion on the police? Malcolm himself said the Black Muslims were trying to kill him, and he was going to

---

Liberty Bell. "Proof" of this bizarre plot was provided by Ray Wood, a Black undercover agent of BOSS (Bureau of Special Services and Investigation—the New York "red squad"). During the course of the trial it became clear that it was Wood, not the defendants, who carried out most of the planning for the "plot." Nevertheless the four activists were convicted in June 1965, and Wood was decorated by the police department.—Ed.

reveal the names of the would-be assassins at the meeting on February 21 where he was murdered."

The above is one response to my article in the July 12 *Militant,* where I took note of certain things printed in the New York newspapers after the assassination that raised questions about the conduct of the police.

The reason I don't "admit" the Black Muslims killed Malcolm is that I don't know that to be a fact. It may be so, but until it is proved it remains only a possibility—one among others. Even if Black Muslims or their agents were out to kill him, they may not have been the only ones. What Malcolm thought about it is important, but not conclusive; he did not have all the facts either.

When his home was bombed on February 14, a week before his assassination, he definitely accused the Black Muslims of the murder attempt. He believed it was a continuation of their bitter attacks and harassments. Once he had made this accusation, it was a perfect setup for other forces to kill him and have it assumed that the Black Muslims were guilty. I do not say it happened that way; I say it could have happened that way if other forces were out to get him.

The police and the press publicized Malcolm's first opinion, but not his later doubts about that opinion. Yet it is a fact that in the last two or three days of his life Malcolm began to have second thoughts about the question. He told associates he was "not all that sure it's the Muslims" and that he was going to quit saying it was.

And in the last hour of his life, as he sat in the small anteroom of the Audubon Ballroom waiting for his turn to speak, he told members of his organization there that he was going to state that he had been hasty to accuse the Black Muslims of bombing his home, because things that had happened after the bombing had convinced him of the existence of a bigger plot, beyond the capabilities of the Black Muslims. Again, he might have been right or he might have been wrong. The point is that he did not know for sure, and therefore his opinion one way or the other is not conclusive.

In the recent Statue of Liberty case in New York, it turned out that the chief initiator of whatever was plotted was an agent provocateur planted there by the city police. When a Ku Klux Klan gang murdered Mrs. Viola Liuzzo in Alabama, it turned out that one member of the gang was an agent planted there by the FBI. It is well known, and Malcolm pointed this out several times, that the police and the FBI have infiltrated the Black Muslims.

These are reasons why I cannot rule out the possibility that a police agent might have been part of the murder gang, even encouraging the plot. It doesn't at all displease the police that Malcolm is dead and his movement beheaded, under circumstances that favor blaming the Black Muslims and possibly wiping out their movement, too.

If such speculation is without basis, if the police did not have an agent in the murder gang, if the police were in no way implicated in the murder, then they should easily be able to clear up the puzzling questions about the second man, whose identity and role they know. While they are at it, perhaps they will clear up some other matters about their conduct.

Malcolm's body was hardly cold before top police officials began bombarding the public with statements about how often they had offered him protection. Every official had a different figure for the number of offers, but all of them said Malcolm refused protection.

Betty Shabazz, Malcolm's widow, had another story. Ted Poston, writing in the February 23 *New York Post*, told of her reaction, the night after the killing, as she was watching TV and heard Deputy Police Commissioner Walter Arm say, "Of course we offered Malcolm X police protection many times—as late as the day his house was bombed." "That's a lie," Mrs. Shabazz said.

Either way, the police are not absolved of the responsibility for preventing murder. They are supposed to protect people, they are supposed to prevent murder, even of people who don't want special protection. And in this case they *knew*, more than a month before February 21, that Malcolm's murder was being planned.

That isn't what I say—that's what they say. "According to the police spokesman, the department knew in mid-January that an attempt was to be made on Malcolm's life," the *New York Journal-American* reported on February 22.

The police spokesman did not say *how* they knew. This would be interesting, but here let us confine ourselves to the question of what the police, knowing about the murder plot, did in and around the Audubon Ballroom on February 21.

We already know that there were "several" undercover police agents in the audience. What about outside? "According to police officials, a patrolman was stationed outside the ballroom," the *New York World-Telegram* reported February 22. A high police official, after confirming that police agents were planted inside the meeting, added, "And there were a couple of uniformed men outside," the *Herald Tribune* reported February 23.

"Deputy Police Commissioner Walter Arm said yesterday [February 22] that a special detail had been assigned outside the ballroom. . . . Assistant Chief Inspector Harry Taylor, in charge of Manhattan North uniformed police said Sunday [February 21] that two sergeants and eighteen patrolmen had been stationed in the area," the *New York Times* reported on February 23.

Which was it—"a" patrolman, "a couple," or a "special detail" of twenty? Why such discrepancies about a relatively simple question? What does it denote—ineptness, indifference, or a sense of guilt?

Let us, for the moment, give the police department the benefit of the doubt and assume that they did assign twenty cops outside the Audubon. The sight of them might have had some effect on the killers. Where were the twenty cops between the time people began to arrive for the rally and the time of the killing? Many witnesses saw few or no cops as they reached the Audubon.

Mrs. Patricia M. Russell, a psychiatric social worker of New Rochelle, who wrote an eyewitness description of the murder in the February 27 *Baltimore Afro-American,* said, "When we drove past the Audubon Ballroom . . . there were two police cars and eight policemen—two in front and six standing across the street at various corners. We had to look for a parking space and did not get back to the ballroom for ten minutes. The area in front of the ballroom was clear of policemen. There was not one officer in sight." This was ten or fifteen minutes before the murder.

Where was the special detail of twenty police at this time?

If it had depended on the cops alone, nobody would have been captured at the scene of the crime. The "several" police agents didn't do anything to catch the men who shot Malcolm down right in front of them. Talmadge Hayer, the only person captured at the Audubon who was indicted by the police for the murder, would have got away if it had depended solely on the cops, inside or outside. Someone shot him in the leg as he fled, and the crowd chasing him caught him outside the ballroom. If it had not been for the shot and the crowd, Hayer would have got away before police showed up.

When the police finally did appear, Hayer was seized from the crowd by Sergeant Alvin Aronoff and Patrolman Louis Angelos. The February 22 *Times* said they "were cruising in their patrol car on upper Broadway shortly after 3 P.M. when they heard shots in the Audubon Ballroom." The February 22 *Daily News* said they "were driving by."

There was no claim by anybody that Aronoff and Angelos belonged to any special detail. They apparently were on regular cruising duty out of their precinct station, and happened to be passing by as Hayer and the people chasing him spilled out into the street.

It is not necessary for me to charge the police with ineptness or indifference—the facts speak for themselves. The question is *why* they acted this way. And related to that question are two others: Did the killers act as boldly as they did because they had reason to believe that none of them would be caught by the police at the Audubon?—which (leaving the second man aside) is exactly how it would have turned out if someone (not a cop) hadn't shot Hayer in the leg. And if they had reason to believe this, what was that reason?

WERE BUTLER AND JOHNSON THERE?

In two previous articles I raised questions about the role of the New York police in the assassination of Malcolm X, and about the indifference of the New York daily press. I am glad to see that I'm not the only one raising questions.

Nat Hentoff, who reviews the press for New York's *Village Voice*, notes in its July 15 issue that "there has been a curious lack of curiosity among the press as to the progress the police have made in investigating the murder and those who hired the guns."

Hentoff reports that a number of questions about the police handling of the case are asked by Alex Haley in his epilogue to *The Autobiography of Malcolm X* (Grove Press). He also refers to Malcolm's "increasing doubts in the days before the assassination that if he were to be murdered, the [Black] Muslims would be responsible.

"Consider the huge press play the assassination received," Hentoff says. "Consider the total silence in recent months. Isn't any editor or reporter at least mildly interested in pursuing the story?"

Apparently not, so far as the New York dailies go. Their curious lack of curiosity and total silence have remained unchanged since Hentoff tried to prod them.

The only response I have seen came from the Harlem weekly, *Amsterdam News*, which printed an article by Les Matthews on July 31 under the title "Malcolm X Murder Is Unsolved." Matthews recounts some well-known facts about the three men indicted for the murder, and offers the opinion that "it is doubtful if the court has a case against the three suspects." But Matthews, unlike the reporters on the big daily papers, at least made inquiries at the office of the district attorney, who is supposed to prosecute murderers. And he got some statements from the wives of two Black Muslims being held for the murder, Norman 3X Butler and Thomas 15X Johnson.

Matthews was told that the grand jury indicted them, along with Talmadge Hayer, "after an investigation by Assistant D.A. Herbert Stein." A spokesman for District Attorney Frank Hogan told the *Amsterdam News* "that Stein is no longer connected with the case and that no Assistant D.A. is currently assigned to it. No date has been set for the trial." The impression left by Matthews's article is that the D.A.'s office no longer seems much concerned about solving the Malcolm X case, if it ever was. Which puts it in the same category as the police department.

Let us return to the role of the police. Less than two hours after Malcolm was shot down, top police officials handed down the line that the killing was the result of a feud between the Black Muslims and Malcolm's movement; that is, the killers were Black Muslims or their agents.

How could they have decided this so fast? How could they be so sure of it that they made no efforts to seek the killers in other quarters?

At the moment of their announcement, they had two men in custody as suspects. One was Talmadge Hayer and the other was an unidentified "second" man—both of whom had been rescued by the police from members of the crowd who thought they were part of the murder gang. At that moment, the police said they had no evidence that Hayer was a Black Muslim or connected with them, and they have not produced any such evidence since that time. The police have never said the "second" man was a Black Muslim; in fact, they have never said anything about him; he just disappeared from sight.

So what evidence did they have for pointing to the Black Muslims so conclusively that they never bothered to investigate any other possibilities?

Malcolm had many enemies besides the Black Muslim leadership. An unbiased investigation would consider *all* the possibilities. To have made that kind of investigation, the police would have had to probe the activities of the FBI, the CIA, *and themselves*—all of whom were hostile to Malcolm and not at all unhappy about his murder.

Could this be the reason why they chose to concentrate their investigation on the Black Muslims, and why after a few days they picked up two well-known Black Muslims and indicted them along with Hayer, for the murder?

Butler and Johnson are well-known Black Muslims, I repeat. In January they and a third man were arrested after an argument with an ex-Muslim, Benjamin Brown, that ended in the shooting of Brown. Butler and Johnson were out on bail on first-degree assault charges in that case at the time of the Malcolm murder. Neither was arrested at the scene or the time of the Malcolm killing. Butler was arrested at his home five days later, on February 26. Johnson was arrested at his home five days after that, on March 3.

The detective's affidavit on which Butler was arrested charged that he, "acting in concert with another previously arrested . . . did assault one Malcolm X Little with guns." The detective's affidavit against Johnson charged that he, "acting in concert with two other males previously arrested . . . did assault one Malcolm X Little with lethal weapons." The grand jury indictment on March 10 charged them and Hayer with willfully killing Malcolm "with a shotgun and pistols."

Now, I don't know if Butler or Johnson had any connection with the murder of Malcolm. I don't know if they had anything to do with its planning. But the charges against them are not that they were connected, etc. The charges are quite specific—that they assaulted Malcolm with weapons, which would mean they had to be in the Audubon Ballroom. *Those* charges I can only greet with considerable skepticism.

My skepticism is not based on the fact that their wives and friends testify they were both at home at the time of the murder. I have no way of judging the validity of the testimony of wives and friends. My skepticism is based on something else.

As I said in my first article, people entering the Audubon on the afternoon of February 21 were not searched, but they were closely scrutinized by Malcolm's assistants and guards. I find it incredible that Butler and Johnson could have gotten into that meeting. They were well-known and leading figures in the New York mosque of the Black Muslims. This means that they were well known to Malcolm's assistants, who had worked side by side with Butler and Johnson less than one year before the assassination.

If Hubert Humphrey was standing at the door to a Cabinet meeting and watching who entered, would Dean Rusk and Robert

McNamara be able to walk past him without his knowing they were going in? It is just as unlikely that Butler and Johnson could have got into the Audubon meeting without being recognized by Malcolm's assistants, and stopped.

Is it any wonder that half a year after the assassination the district attorney's office considers the case against Butler and Johnson so weak that it doesn't even have an assistant D.A. assigned to it any more?

There is another aspect of the case that cries out for investigation.

On February 9, or twelve days before he was killed, Malcolm arrived in France to speak at a meeting to which he had been invited. He had spoken in Paris the previous November without incident. But this time he was banned as "undesirable."

Malcolm assumed, and said, that the French authorities had excluded him because they feared and disliked his role in organizing Afro-Americans and African groups in Paris.

But I have heard—third-hand—that after the assassination Malcolm's associates expressed the belief that the reason for his being excluded was that the French government thought he might be assassinated on French soil, and did not want to bear the onus for such a scandal.

I stress this is third-hand; it is unverified, a rumor. But it seems to me the kind of rumor that deserves serious follow-up. France does not often bar American citizens whose papers are in order, and it tolerates a considerable variety of political activity up to a certain point. Malcolm's assumption about the reason for his being banned could be wrong.

On the other hand, if the rumor is true, then further light might be cast on the identity of the killers by discovering *why* the French authorities believed Malcolm might be killed while in Paris; *who* gave them reason to believe it; if they were actually told that the Black Muslims have the resources to organize a murder in France, etc.

The French government might not cooperate with an investigation of such questions, and if it did cooperate its answers might not add anything to present knowledge about the murder. But as Nat Hentoff asked, "Isn't any editor or reporter at least mildly interested in pursuing the story?" And if not, why not?

3

The trial

by Herman Porter

Herman Porter attended the whole Malcolm X murder trial in New York, from January 21 to March 11, 1966. These nine articles were printed in the Militant, January 24–March 21, 1966.

SELECTION OF THE JURY

New York, January 18—Nine jurors have been selected thus far during the five days that the Supreme Court has actually been proceeding with the trial of the three men accused of murdering Malcolm X.

The indictment was read by Assistant District Attorney Vincent J. Dermody at the start of the selection on January 12. It charges the defendants with murder in the first degree, and alleges that the defendants—Thomas Hagan, also known as Talmadge Hayer, twenty-two; Norman Butler, twenty-six; and Thomas Johnson, thirty—"willfully, feloniously, and with malice aforethought" shot and killed Malcolm X with a shotgun and pistols at the Audubon Ballroom on February 21, 1965.

In questioning prospective jurors, Dermody repeatedly asked whether testimony that any or each of the defendants was a member of the Black Muslims would prejudice the juror. William C. Chance, one of the two court-appointed attorneys for Butler, objected to these references to the Black Muslims. He said that no group was on trial, only the three defendants.

Several prospective jurors were asked by defense attorneys whether they would give any more credence to the testimony of a member of the FBI or the CIA than to other witnesses.

Each of the defendants has two lawyers. Those representing Butler (Chance and Joseph B. Williams) and those representing Johnson (Joseph Pinckney and Charles T. Beavers) are court appointed. All four are Negroes. Hagan has retained his own lawyers: Peter L. F. Sabbatino and Peter Yellin, both white.

The press has generally reported that all three defendants have been identified as Black Muslims. Hagan, however, was not known as a Black Muslim and was not reported to be a member at the time of his arrest. His attorney reportedly denies Hagan was ever a member of the Muslims. Hagan was shot in the leg and apprehended at the Audubon Ballroom at the time of the assassination. Butler and Johnson were arrested some days later.

Spectators have been barred from the court during the selection of the jurors. The reason given is that there is no room for spectators because of the large panel of prospective jurors waiting to be called. However, barring of spectators is said to be an unusual practice.

The trial was originally to have begun December 6 but was adjourned by Judge Charles Marks because of the Christmas holiday until January 3. The transit strike caused a further postponement.

Although there were only about a dozen Negroes in a panel of approximately 100 in the courtroom, the first two jurors selected are Negroes. George S. Carter, a chemist, automatically became foreman of the jury when he was chosen as the first juror. Reginald H. Brent, the second juror, is a subway motorman. The other jurors are: Mrs. Sophie Belenky, retired from the jewelry business; Robert P. Hixon, a signal maintenance man with the transit authority; Frederick R. Caruso, linotype operator for the *Journal American;*

Gerald M. Sullivan, on the staff of a sales department; Mrs. Veronica L. Camilletti, a housewife; Vincent T. LaPiano, a sanitation worker in Harlem; and Thomas Makwcewicz, a draftsman.

The defendants face a possible sentence of life in prison if convicted. New York State eliminated the death penalty in 1965.

THE FIRST WITNESS

New York, January 25—The trial of the three men accused of murdering Malcolm X began with the opening statement by the prosecution, presented to the jury on January 21. Vincent J. Dermody, the assistant district attorney in charge of the prosecution, explained that an opening statement in which the prosecutor states what he expects to prove in the case is required by law. A summary of Dermody's statement follows:

In 1952 Malcolm X became a member of the Black Muslims, which was under the leadership of Elijah Muhammad. Malcolm X became a minister and established Mosque No. 7 in Harlem. On November 23, 1963, Malcolm X was suspended from his duties as a minister and remained suspended thereafter. In March 1964 Malcolm X broke away from the Black Muslims and formed his own organization. It was known as the Organization of Afro-American Unity and also as the Muslim Mosque, Incorporated, and had its headquarters at the Hotel Theresa. He attracted many people, including Black Muslims. He held weekly rallies, invariably at the Audubon Ballroom.

On February 21, 1965, at about 3 p.m., Malcolm X started to address an audience of about 200 people at the Audubon. The three defendants, all active members of the Black Muslims, were in the auditorium. Talmadge Hayer (also known as Thomas Hagan) and Norman 3X Butler were seated together, each with an automatic pistol. Thomas 15X Johnson was seated alone, with a shotgun.

By a prearranged plan, Hayer and Butler created a disturbance. Hayer shouted about Butler trying to pick his pocket. At this point Johnson approached the stage and fired point blank at Malcolm X. In the confusion, Hayer and Butler rushed toward the stage and each fired shots into the prone body of Malcolm X. Johnson dropped the shotgun on the floor and slipped away. Hayer and Butler were pursued by several people but Butler managed to escape. Hayer was shot in the leg; he was caught and beaten. Police rescued him.

An autopsy showed that Malcolm X died of pellets from a shotgun, and bullets from a .45 caliber automatic and a 9 mm automatic. Police recovered the weapons and ballistics experts will testify that they were the ones used to kill Malcolm X.

Butler was arrested February 25, 1965, and Johnson was arrested March 3.

The defense attorneys have the option of also making an opening statement. Only Peter L.F. Sabbatino, Hayer's lawyer, chose to do so. In brief, Sabbatino said that he would show the following: Hayer was arrested on February 21 and held incommunicado for almost three weeks. He was not arraigned or brought into a court of law for several weeks. He was not allowed to see an attorney or any member of his family during that time.

Hayer denies categorically that he was a member of the Muslim movement, said Sabbatino. He went to the Audubon Ballroom alone and out of curiosity. The person who shot him, Sabbatino said, had a criminal record and would naturally seek to claim in self-defense that Hayer shot Malcolm X. The identification of Hayer as one of the assassins was by a mob, he concluded.

Testimony of the first important eyewitness, Cary Thomas, began the same day, after a presentation of diagrams of the building and auditorium in which the shooting took place. Cross-examination of Thomas is not yet completed after his third day on the witness stand.

In response to Dermody's questions, Thomas testified that he had witnessed the murder and seen it unfold just as Dermody's opening statement said it had. Thomas said he knew the three defendants to be Muslims and had seen each of them several times in Harlem's Mosque No. 7.

Thomas told the following story: He had seen Johnson sitting at the back of the ballroom when he arrived at about 2:20 p.m. on

Launching the Organization of Afro-American Unity.
Audubon Ballroom, Harlem, June 28, 1964.

In Cairo, July 17, 1964. Malcolm suspected the U.S.
government tried to poison him there.

THE AUDUBON BALLROOM
Diagram of the Assassination

Prosecution version:

(1) Two men (Hayer and Butler) scuffle, diverting Malcolm's guards (G).

(2) A smoke bomb goes off in rear. [Gene Roberts, one of guards closest to bomb, is a New York police undercover agent.]

(3) A man (Johnson) moves forward, shotguns Malcolm X.

(4) The two men who scuffled run to stage, shoot Malcolm with pistols.

(5) Two assassins flee to rear. One (Hayer) is caught by crowd. The others escape.

Talmadge Hayer's confession:

(1) One man in rear diverts guards with smoke bomb and scuffle.

(2) Hayer and another man are in first row, with pistols.

(3) A fourth man uses shotgun.

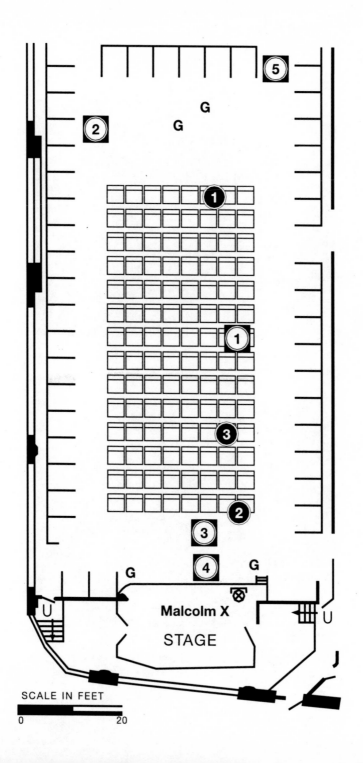

SCALE IN FEET

0   20

The crowd captures Talmadge Hayer. Police rescue him outside the Audubon Ballroom.

Gene Roberts unsuccessfully attempts mouth-to-mouth resuscitation. Years later he surfaced as undercover police agent.

Police Hint:

MALCOLM'S

KILLERS

BULLETIN

Police investigating the assassination of Malcolm X are "on the right track" toward solution of the slaying, Asst. Chief Inspector Joseph L. Coyle said today.

Coyle, who commands Manhattan North Detectives and is in charge of the investigation, said he would confer with District Attorney Hogan's office today in connection with the investigation. He declined to say why.

It was reported that police know the names of all five men who formed the murder team.

(Earlier story on Page 3.)

KNOWN

New York Post reports "police know the names of all five men who formed the murder team," February 24, 1965. A week later, after arrest of three suspects (below), the investigation is stopped.

Hayer   Butler   Johnson

February 21. He went over to Reuben Francis after he saw Johnson. When Malcolm X began to address the audience, Thomas was seated in a booth on the left side of the chairs which faced the stage. Hayer rose from his chair directly in front of where Thomas was sitting. Hayer said: "Man, what are you doing with your hands in my pocket?" to Butler, who was seated next to Hayer. Hayer had an automatic pistol in his hand. He turned and faced Thomas directly.

Then there was a gunshot and Thomas saw a man standing near Malcolm X facing the stage. The man turned around and Thomas saw it was Johnson holding a sawed-off shotgun. After that, Hayer and Butler ran toward the stage. Thomas saw them both at the stage with their backs toward him. Each was making the same pumping motion with his hand, as if firing a gun. Though he had never actually seen a gun in Butler's hand, he saw "shells being ejected from the pistol falling on the floor."

Cary Thomas has stuck to this story through all the cross-examination so far. Though he is doggedly certain about his observation of these events and his memory of them, his knowledge of the other circumstances surrounding the assassination is extremely faulty, and his memory of almost everything else about which he was questioned connected with the case is outrageously bad.

Thomas described his background under questioning by the defense: He has also been known as Abdul Malik and Cary 2X. He is thirty-five, married, with four children, but had not seen his wife during the two years before the assassination.

He has owned at least one gun ever since he was fifteen and usually carried one on his person. He had one with him at the Audubon but did not use it then. He was in the army from 1947 to 1953 and was court-martialed some ten times, sometimes for serious crimes like possession of a pistol with intent to do bodily harm. He was discharged for bad conduct.

He was a user of heroin for three years, and a pusher. He was convicted of possession of narcotics in 1961 in Boston. The two-year sentence was suspended and he was placed on probation.

Thomas said that he joined the Black Muslims. He testified first that he joined officially and received his X from Chicago in December 1963, and left in November 1964. Later he said he didn't recall the date he joined. At another time he testified that he had never been in Mosque No. 7, where he was a member, after November 1963.

He testified that he couldn't remember whether Malcolm X was the minister when he joined. There were several ministers, he said, but he couldn't remember the names of any of them. One time he said he attended meetings for about one year before he joined. Another time he stated that he'd been going for two years.

Thomas declared that he left the Black Muslims when Malcolm X did. He said he was a member of Malcolm's organization for about a year. (Malcolm X was killed not quite one year after he broke with Elijah Muhammad.) But Thomas never discovered that Malcolm formed two organizations—one religious, the Muslim Mosque, Incorporated, and one non-religious but dedicated to winning "freedom, justice, and equality" for black people in America, the Organization of Afro-American Unity. He still thinks they are the same organization—that the OAAU was partly religious—even though Malcolm X made the distinction repeatedly. The OAAU was not formed until many months after the Muslim Mosque, which was an orthodox Islamic organization.

Though Thomas claimed to be a member of the Black Muslims, his testimony showed he didn't act like one. He remained separated from his wife and children during the entire period, even though the Muslims place stress on the importance of family life. He testified he was sent to Bellevue Hospital (which is often used for psychiatric observation) because he was drunk. This incident occurred in 1963 after he supposedly joined the Muslims. Muslims have a strict taboo against alcohol.

The most important contradiction revealed so far in Thomas's testimony involves a reversal of the roles of the defendants in his story. According to records read at the trial, Thomas testified before the grand jury on March 3, 1965, that *Johnson* and Butler, not Hayer and Butler, rushed toward the stage after the shotgun blast. Thomas claims that this was a slip made because he was nervous and in fear of his life. At the time of the assassination, the police told the press that *Hayer* was the one who had fired the shotgun. When they changed their minds is not clear.

In his testimony before the grand jury, Thomas identified Hayer as a member of the Jersey City mosque. Under cross-examination he revealed that the only basis for this was that he had seen Hayer with members of the Jersey City mosque several times. He could not recall the dates, even approximately, when he had seen any of the three defendants in the Harlem mosque, though he claimed to have seen each of them several times.

Thomas was picked up on March 2, 1965, and held by police as a material witness. While in jail he was indicted for arson and transferred on June 4 to a regular prison in Queens.

UNRELIABLE OBSERVERS

New York, February 1—Five eyewitnesses have testified so far in the trial of three men accused of murdering Malcolm X, but not much light has been shed on some of the questions surrounding the case.

The prosecution alleges that Malcolm X was shot by three active members of the Black Muslims on February 21 at the Audubon Ballroom, presumably because of his split from and differences with Elijah Muhammad. Two of the defendants, Norman 3X Butler and Thomas 15X Johnson, are well-known Muslims—according to the press, "enforcers." How could they have even been in the ballroom when Malcolm's followers, who knew them, observed each person entering and checked the auditorium for possible attackers?

Talmadge Hayer, also known as Thomas Hagan, the only defendant caught at the scene of the assassination, denies he was ever a Muslim. And he was not publicly known to be a Muslim. He was shot at the scene, allegedly by Reuben Francis, one of Malcolm X's guards. If he was one of the attackers but not a Black Muslim, that opens the question of who organized the assassination. There are other powerful groups besides the Black Muslims who were very anxious to be rid of Malcolm X—including the U.S. ruling class.

Cary Thomas, the first witness, who testified for three and a half days, was the only one to identify all the defendants in the ballroom and to say he knew them all to be members of the Black Muslims. On January 27 the transcript of the testimony he gave to the grand jury on March 3, 1965, was read into the record. The account of the attack he gave the grand jury was quite different from the one he gave at the trial.

The differences between his two stories, as well as many other discrepancies, throw doubt on the truth of his testimony. He said, for example, that after the shooting started he got up from the booth he was sitting in, some forty-five feet from the stage, and walked forward to within fifteen feet, or possibly seven or eight feet or even less from the stage, where Butler and Hagan were standing pumping bullets into Malcolm X. He never drew his gun, even though the assassins had their backs toward him, because he was afraid he might hit other people running around. Instead he got down on the floor in one of the booths.

Thomas claimed to see Johnson when he first entered the ballroom, and to recognize him as a Black Muslim. But he did nothing to prevent this presumed enemy from attacking Malcolm X. The scrutiny the audience was subjected to by Malcolm's followers was reflected in the testimony of George Whitney, the fourth witness. A report of police questioning of him on March 2, 1965, was read into the record. Whitney told the police that when he noticed a member of the Muslims from Paterson, New Jersey, in the audience he went and spoke with him. The man said he was there because he was dissatisfied with the Black Muslims. Two guards then went over to him. They had him remove his Black Muslim pin and allowed him to return to his seat, Whitney said. The question of how Muslims in the audience were treated was not probed by any of the attorneys, however.

Whitney testified that he had been a member of Mosque No. 7 for two and a half years and had known Butler for three years. He said he did not see Butler in the Audubon on February 21, and that he would have recognized him if he had.

Whitney, who lives in the same apartment building as Cary Thomas and had known him for fifteen years, testified that he had joined both of Malcolm's organizations, the Organization for Afro-American Unity and the Muslim Mosque, Incorporated. He seemed to have a much better grasp of what they were about than Cary Thomas. When asked whether Malcolm X had ever said who was interested in gunning him down, Whitney testified that Malcolm said that the power structure and the Black Muslims were both interested in his death.

Hayer was the only one of the defendants Whitney identified. He said, in fact, that he was the first one to catch hold of Hayer as he was fleeing the ballroom. Whitney was walking up the center aisle away from the stage when the shooting started. He saw two figures running back toward him—jumping over chairs and telling people to get out of the way. He got a look at only one of them, and saw him fire twice with a large gun that looked like a .45. Whitney moved toward the man but jumped out of his way when the man fired in his direction. The man passed within only two feet and Whitney pursued him out the entrance and down the stairs. He caught Hayer five or six feet outside the entrance of the building. Others also grabbed him.

Assistant District Attorney Dermody produced an automatic pistol which Whitney said looked like the one he'd seen in Hayer's hand. Whitney testified that he didn't realize Hayer had been shot when he caught him, and that he never saw anyone fire at Hayer. Hayer's attorney has alleged repeatedly that Reuben Francis shot Hayer, and he suggested in a question that Whitney's testimony was motivated by his desire to protect Francis.

Whitney was incarcerated on March 10, 1965, and accused of shooting a man on March 9. He was held on $50,000 bail, then held without bail, then on $10,000 bail, and was finally released November 23. He was also accused of shooting a woman, on the same day as the other shooting, it seems, but that charge has been dismissed, he said.

Whitney was not due to appear as a witness, and he never testified before the grand jury. He appeared in court as a spectator on

January 24 after Cary Thomas had mentioned his name. Someone informed Peter Sabbatino, Hayer's lawyer, that Whitney was in the courtroom and Sabbatino asked to have him put on the witness stand. The prosecution called him as a witness a few days later.

Two other eyewitnesses who testified proved themselves to be very unreliable observers in the course of cross-examination.

Vernal Temple, twenty-three years old, had difficulty in hearing and understanding many of the questions. He testified that he knew Johnson as "15X" and had seen him sitting near the back of the Audubon Ballroom on February 21. The only other time he had seen 15X was at a big Muslim rally he had attended in Chicago—but he could not recall anything else about the trip, the name of the bus line he used, the fare, or the time it took.

Most of his testimony concerned Hayer. He said that he was seated on the right side of the auditorium when a man stood up and said: "Nigger, get out of my pocket." He recognized him to be Hayer, though he pronounced his name as "Hangan," meaning to say "Hagan." Temple said he had seen Hayer on three previous occasions: first, selling *Muhammad Speaks* at Lenox Avenue and 116th Street, near Mosque No. 7; second, in the mosque acting as a guard; third, in the Muslim restaurant.

Temple's reliability as a witness was shaken by a question put to him by Dermody after the defense cross-examination was over. Dermody asked Temple for the date on which President Kennedy was assassinated. Temple responded that he wasn't sure of the exact date but he knew it was in 1965.

The fourth eyewitness, Edward DiPina, was a man of seventy, black but of Portuguese birth. A very likable old man, he tried to please his questioner and tended to answer "yes" when he was unsure. He had difficulty in understanding many questions and in answering them directly.

He identified Butler and Hayer as being involved in the disturbance, but the rest of the story he told was different from that of the others: Butler and Hayer were in the third row from the front. Butler stood up and fired five shots at Malcolm X on the stage. Then he and Hayer turned around and ran toward the rear of the auditorium, firing behind them. In DiPina's version, they never ran forward to the stage as the other witnesses testified.

Though there were many things DiPina said which showed his confusion in spite of very positive assertions, one stood out: William Chance, Butler's attorney, asked him about the detective who drove DiPina to Bellevue Hospital where he first identified Hayer. Then he pointed to Charles Beavers, one of Johnson's attorneys, requested him to stand up, and asked DiPina if that was the man who took him to the hospital. "Yes, that's the man," responded DiPina.

The fifth eyewitness, who has not yet been cross-examined, is Jasper Davis, a fifty-four-year-old superintendent of an apartment building. He said he was not a member of any of the organizations involved. He identified only Butler, as one of the two involved in the diversion, but he did not see who fired any of the shots.

CONFLICTING TESTIMONY

New York, February 8—During thirteen days of testimony in the Malcolm X murder trial, nine eyewitnesses to the assassination of Malcolm X have taken the stand and been cross-examined at length. But little progress has been made toward discovering the truth about what happened on February 21, 1965, in the Audubon Ballroom where Malcolm X was shot, and the motive behind the assassination.

A complicating factor in the trial is the crucial role in the proceedings played by the police and district attorney's office. Though they are the ones who represent "the people," they can hardly be considered impartial, and some people suspect agents of the police were implicated in the murder.

The most powerful people who run this country had a motive for having Malcolm X murdered at least as strong as that of the hierarchy of the Black Muslims. And they were in a much better position to get away with it. Right-wing and racist groups had motives as well.

In the last speech he delivered, at the Audubon Ballroom on Monday, February 15, the day after his house had been bombed, Malcolm X accused Elijah Muhammad of ordering the bombing of his home, but he went on to say that a situation had been created in which *anyone* could murder him and the Black Muslims would be blamed.

Alex Haley reports in the epilogue to *The Autobiography of Malcolm X* that Malcolm told him in a phone conversation on February 20 that he was going to state he had been hasty to accuse the Black Muslims of bombing his home. "Things have happened since that are bigger than what they can do. I know what they can do. Things have gone beyond that," Haley quotes Malcolm.

More than any other individual, Malcolm X was a threat to those who wish to maintain the status quo in this country. Peter Sabbatino, one of the defense attorneys for Talmadge Hayer, asked George Whitney, one of Malcolm's followers, during the cross-examination, whether he ever heard Malcolm say that people interested in narcotics might gun him down. "He said that people who were interested in keeping the status quo might gun him down," Whitney responded.

Malcolm X made an enormous impression in Africa during the last year of his life. Once he split from the Muslims, only eleven months before his death, the goal he set was to link the struggle of Afro-Americans to the freedom struggles of the nonwhite peoples all over the world. His immediate aim was to get the U.S. government condemned as racist in the United Nations, just as South Africa had been condemned.

He spent five of those eleven months traveling in Africa and the Middle East, meeting heads of state and high government officials and speaking before student groups. A "truth squad" from the U.S. Information Agency accompanied him wherever he went—slandering him and trying to undo what he was accomplishing. But they didn't succeed. John Lewis and Donald Harris, leaders of the Student Nonviolent Coordinating Committee, toured several African countries just after Malcolm had visited them and reported:

"Malcolm's impact on Africa was just fantastic. In every country he was known and served as the main criteria for categorizing other Afro-Americans and their political views."

Malcolm X was poisoned while he was in Cairo. His stomach was pumped very soon after he awoke one night in enormous pain. No one else who ate with him was poisoned. He mentioned the incident, during the question period at one of the public meetings of the Organization of Afro-American Unity at the Audubon Ballroom, in an off-hand way. He was probably embarrassed to speak of his own problems, especially when he was so widely accused by the press of being just a publicity hound.

Just twelve days before his assassination, Malcolm X was barred from France. He was to address a meeting of Afro-Americans and Africans in Paris and flew there, but was kept from leaving the airport and forced to fly directly back to Britain by French officials. The reason for this highly unusual act by the French government was never stated, but one rumor was that they feared they would be embarrassed by having him assassinated on French soil.

One other rumor that should be taken note of in another connection was spread among some New York policemen: that Malcolm X's group had become an organized criminal gang. I don't know who started to spread this lie or how long before the assassination it was told to police, but it certainly must have "justified" any attacks on Malcolm or his followers to those police who believed the story.

For all of these reasons, there are grounds for suspicion that some agency of the government was involved in one way or another in the assassination, and that those charged with finding the killers may indeed be covering up for them.

The police must have interviewed a great many of the estimated 400 people who were at the Audubon when Malcolm was shot. Did they select the witnesses who could be fitted into the prosecution's story? Some had seen a small part of what happened and couldn't contradict the rest of the prosecution's version. Were others subjected to pressure by the police, to learn to remember what the police wanted? Other witnesses were confused but open to suggestion by the authorities.

Newspaper accounts of the killing at the time said at least five men were involved in the attack—two in a diversion and three doing the shooting. The police said they were looking for five men. The prosecution now claims only three men were involved, and none of the witnesses has contradicted that in court.

Two of them, however, testified before the grand jury last spring to a course of events involving more than three assassins. The last witness to testify, Charles Blackwell, is one of them. Blackwell was a guard standing in front of the stage, on the left side from the point of view of the audience, at the time of the shooting. He seemed like a very sober, serious, reliable witness as he testified in court to seeing most of the action unfold; and he told it in court just as Assistant District Attorney Dermody said it had happened:

When a scuffle between two men started, Blackwell moved toward the middle aisle, he said. When he reached the first row he heard a blast behind him and saw Malcolm X fall. Then he heard shots, turned, and saw the two men who had been scuffling running down the aisle toward him, shooting at Malcolm X. Blackwell identified the two as the defendants Norman 3X Butler and Talmadge Hayer, also known as Thomas Hagan. Butler pointed his gun at Blackwell and Blackwell ducked to the floor. They both ran past him toward the rostrum, then turned and ran up the aisle, Blackwell testified. He "gave chase" and then he noticed a man standing four or five rows back who turned and ran into the ladies' lounge. Blackwell identified that man as Thomas 15X Johnson, the third defendant.

Blackwell's account of the events before the grand jury on March 9, 1965, however, was very different, although he identified the same three men. According to this story: Two men started to scuffle. Then something went "pop." It seemed to come from the back of the auditorium. This was followed by a volley of shots, but Blackwell did not see where they came from. Then Butler and Hayer, who were not involved in the scuffle but had been sitting in the first and second seats of the first row, ran up the aisle toward the back where the exit was, shooting over people's heads. He testified that he saw Johnson run into the ladies' room. He could not identify the two men in the scuffle. But it was clear from this testimony before the grand jury that there were two others besides the three defendants he identified.

When he was questioned about the discrepancies Blackwell testified that he had lied before the grand jury, because he was ashamed he had left his post, and did not want anyone to know he had ducked down when one of the assassins pointed his gun at him.

Blackwell said that after the shooting Fred Williams, the previous witness to testify against Butler and Johnson, pointed out a sawed-off shotgun and a German Luger lying on the floor. Blackwell wrapped the shotgun in his brown suit jacket and gave it to Reuben Francis, who was standing on the stage at the time, he explained. Then he picked up a jacket he found on the floor, wrapped the Luger in it, and gave this to Francis as well. According to his grand jury testimony, Blackwell gave the Luger to a Brother Gene[*], who was also on the stage. Blackwell claimed he was in error when he said this before the grand jury.

The witness testified that he left the auditorium along with Francis and a third man whose car they drove around in for several hours. Francis told him he had left the shotgun in the ballroom behind the stage. The shotgun he identified in the courtroom is double-barreled, but in his grand jury testimony Blackwell described the weapon as single-barreled with one trigger; however, he said he had not examined it closely. It looked like an old-fashioned dueling pistol, he said. He was not sure it was a sawed-off shotgun because he'd never seen one before.

The other witness whose grand jury testimony involved more than three attackers is Cary Thomas. The story he told on March 3 be-

---

[*] "Brother Gene" was Gene Roberts, an agent of the New York police (BOSS) who surfaced in 1970 as the star witness against thirteen Black Panthers in a conspiracy trial. They were eventually acquitted of charges of plotting to blow up Macy's, Bloomingdale's, the Bronx Botanical Gardens, and other targets.—Ed.

fore the grand jury is, in brief, as follows: Hayer and Butler created a disturbance. Hayer became involved in a fight with some of Malcolm X's followers, while Butler and Johnson rushed to the stage and fired guns at Malcolm. Johnson's gun was identified as a hand gun and Thomas did not mention seeing anyone fire a shotgun. Presumably that was fired by a fourth assailant.

The story the prosecution said it would prove involving only three assailants is extremely dubious on the face of it. Why would two of the three killers deliberately attract attention to themselves before they ran down to the stage with guns firing? This would hardly serve as a diversion if they themselves were the gunmen.

Did they have sufficient time after the two shotgun blasts to run down to the stage? The defense attorneys have not probed this question.

Another important part of the prosecution's case which rings false to those familiar with the situation is the claim that the three men were active members of the Black Muslims, and that their motive for killing Malcolm X was his defection from the Muslims. If the Black Muslims decided to kill Malcolm X, would they send Johnson and Butler, two well-known local "enforcers" who had associated with Malcolm X and his followers for years?

The defense attorneys have not fully utilized the opportunities they had thus far to make the situation clear to the jury. John Davis, who testified to seeing Hayer run toward the exit firing a pistol, was in charge of posting the guards at the stage. None of the lawyers for Butler or Johnson cross-examined him about the precautions taken to prevent known Muslims from entering the ballroom to attack Malcolm, though they must realize such precautions were taken.

Hayer's attorney failed to bring out the fact that Blackwell would have known Hayer if Hayer had been a member of the Black Muslims. Blackwell testified he was a member of the Black Muslims from 1959 to 1964 and a lieutenant at the Jersey City mosque. He did not know Hayer, however, when he saw him at the Audubon Ballroom. Cary Thomas testified Hayer was a member of the Jersey City mosque. Hayer denies he was ever a Muslim.

The question of whether or not Hayer is a Muslim is important in finding out the truth about the assassination. Hayer was not publicly known as a Muslim in Paterson, New Jersey, where he lived. At the time of Malcolm's death, Hayer had been out on bail for about a year on the charge of having robbed a gun store of some forty weapons. He was shot and captured by the crowd at the scene of the killing. Six witnesses so far—among them George Whitney and John Davis, who were closely associated with Malcolm X and had no inconsistencies in their testimony—said they saw Hayer firing a gun. The weight of evidence thus far indicates that he is a gunman, hired or forced to participate in the murder, but not a member of the Black Muslims.

If that is true, it raises the next question: Who hired him or pressured him to commit murder? The defense attorneys have also failed to raise any question about the second suspect who was rescued from the audience and taken into custody by Patrolman Thomas Hoy in the Audubon Ballroom. This second suspect disappeared from the pages of the press. The first accounts mentioned him, but later stories dropped any mention of his being taken into custody.

One of the witnesses to testify on February 4 was Alvin Aronoff, the policeman who was on radio patrol and happened by the Audubon at the time of the murder. He testified that he rescued Hayer from the crowd outside the Audubon and then arrested him. He said he didn't see the crowd attacking any other suspect.

Surely the defense must be interested in who the second suspect is. They might have begun to find out by questioning Aronoff about the policeman who was reported to have taken the suspect into custody. But they haven't questioned the witnesses about a second man being caught by the crowd.

William Chance, attorney for Butler, has taken a different approach entirely. Some of his questions have been aimed at showing that there was dissension in Malcolm's organization between those who wanted to stress religious activities and those who were interested in politics. He has suggested that some of Malcolm X's own followers were interested in doing away with their leader because of these differences.

One of the witnesses at the trial was allowed by the judge to testify in secret. All spectators, including the press, were excluded from the court.

So far testimony has been taken from eight eyewitnesses who testified in open court, one who testified secretly, one policeman who arrived at the entrance to the building after the shooting, and a civil engineer who constructed a diagram of the auditorium and one of the building. Apparently there are many more prosecution witnesses to come, and the defense may have a number of witnesses as well. It remains to be seen if the questions raised in this article will be answered as the trial progresses.

TECHNICAL EVIDENCE

New York, February 15—A series of detectives and technical witnesses have testified during the past week in the trial of the three men accused of murdering Malcolm X. The most important piece of evidence to emerge from all this testimony is the identification of a fingerprint of Talmadge Hayer, also known as Thomas Hagan, one of the defendants, on a crude device set aflame in the Audubon Ballroom at the time of the shooting.

Roland B. Wallace, a thirty-eight-year-old member of the Organization of Afro-American Unity, testified on February 10 that he had just reentered the ballroom at the rear when shots rang out. Then his attention was attracted to a burning "smoke bomb." It was near a window at the rear on the right side facing the stage. Someone poured water on it and put it out.

Detective John J. Keeley testified that he found the wet device, a man's sock stuffed with matches and other material, later in the afternoon of February 21, 1965, near where Wallace had seen it. He turned it over to Detective Edward Meagher, who examined it for fingerprints and other evidence. Meagher took the witness stand next and said he found a usable fingerprint on a piece of unravelled film that was in the sock. He found no usable fingerprints on the shotgun or .45 caliber automatic that have been entered into evidence thus far in the trial.

Detective Robert Meyer testified on February 11 that the fingerprint on the film and one taken from the left thumb of Hayer were "one and the same."

Dr. Milton Helpern, the city's chief medical examiner, took the stand the same day and described the results of the autopsy he had performed on the body of Malcolm X. The cause of death was multiple shotgun pellet and bullet wounds in the chest, heart, and aorta, he said. Malcolm X was hit by eight shotgun slugs and nine bullets from .45 caliber and 9 mm guns. The evidence indicated he was hit by the shotgun slugs while standing and by bullets from the other weapons while prone.

On February 14 Detective James A. Scaringe, a ballistics expert, described a great many slugs and shells found at the scene of the assassination. Aside from the three types mentioned above, three .32 caliber bullets were found near the ballroom office door.

On the morning of February 9 the second secret witness of the trial gave his testimony. The court was cleared of spectators and reporters before he appeared. Reportedly this witness is an FBI agent who was given the .45 caliber automatic that Hayer is alleged by the first secret witness to have used.

According to reliable sources the first secret witness testified on February 3 that he picked up the .45 at the Audubon Ballroom and turned it over to the FBI. He identified Norman 3X Butler and at least one of the two other defendants.

Detective Ferdinand Cavallaro, who was originally in charge of the investigation, was questioned at length about a list of 119 names of people questioned concerning the case when he testified on February 9.

During his cross-examination by Hayer's attorney, Cavallaro mentioned that Reuben Francis, who was indicted for shooting Hayer but later disappeared, had been rearrested on February 2, 1966, in Assistant District Attorney Dermody's office. A spokesman for the district attorney's office said that Francis had been picked up by the FBI. He had forfeited $10,000 bail, and was now being held on $25,000 bail. A spokesman for the FBI denied any knowledge of Francis.

The number of spectators at the trial has dwindled over the weeks. Spectators are still being subjected to the practice of being frisked each time they enter the courtroom.

DEFENSE OPENS CASE

New York, February 22—After twenty days of testimony, the prosecution finished the presentation of its case February 18 against the three men accused of assassinating Malcolm X. Yesterday, the defense began with opening statements on behalf of two of the defendants, Norman 3X Butler and Thomas 15X Johnson.

William Chance, Butler's attorney, said that they will prove that Butler was not at the Audubon Ballroom on February 21, 1965, when Malcolm X was gunned down. Butler does not know Talmadge Hayer (also known as Thomas Hagan), the defendant who was shot and caught at the scene, Chance asserted. The defense will show that the circumstances of the killing made it impossible or improbable for Butler to have participated. Lastly, they will show that Butler had no motive for killing Malcolm X, Chance concluded.

Charles Beavers, one of Johnson's attorneys, said they would show that Johnson was in another county at the time Malcolm X was shot, and that Johnson had no reason whatsoever to participate in the murder.

The presentation of defense witnesses for Hayer began after the opening statements. Three of Hayer's relatives—LeRoi A. Mosely, his brother-in-law; Mrs. Cathleen Mosely, his step-sister; and Horace E. Hayer, his brother—testified briefly. Each of them said that Hayer had never shown any interest in the Muslims or black nationalism. Hayer has maintained that he was never a member of the Muslims. Though the first two eyewitnesses to testify, Cary Thomas and Vernal Temple, claimed to know that Hayer was a Muslim, their generally unreliable testimony was especially weak on this point.

The question of what protection the police provided for Malcolm

X has never been raised at the trial, but considerable light was shed on this by the testimony of Patrolman Gilbert Henry, one of the last prosecution witnesses, on February 17. Henry, a Negro, and his partner, Patrolman John Carroll, were assigned to the Audubon Ballroom on the day Malcolm X was murdered. At almost all previous meetings held by Malcolm X at the Audubon, uniformed policemen were stationed at the entrance to the building—usually about a half dozen of them. But on this occasion—just a week after Malcolm's home had been fire bombed and burned to the ground in such a way that Malcolm and his family were nearly trapped inside—the two policemen were told to conceal themselves.

They were stationed in the Rose Room—not the main auditorium where the meeting was held. They were instructed to remain where they could not be seen and, if anything happened, to summon help with a walkie-talkie they had with them. The other walkie-talkie was in the hands of police stationed in Presbyterian Medical Center, a complex of buildings on the other side of a broad avenue.

When Patrolman Henry heard shots he called on the walkie-talkie but got no answer. He ran into the main auditorium, he said, but saw no one with a gun. There were no other uniformed policemen in the ballroom, nor did he recognize any detectives, Henry testified.

When asked about what efforts he had made to get the names of witnesses, Henry said he had asked about two people for their names but had been unable to get the name of anyone.

Mrs. Betty Shabazz, Malcolm X's widow, testified earlier that day. She had been occupied with her children during the shooting and was unable to identify any of the assassins. She left the witness stand after answering a few routine questions. Obviously upset, she paused near the three defendants. When a guard urged her on out of the courtroom she said: "They killed my husband. They killed him."

Charles Moore, who said he was self-employed and did public relations work, testified on February 18. He said he was sitting in a booth at the right-hand side of the auditorium facing the stage near the rear when a commotion began. He got up and when the shooting started saw a man standing with an automatic weapon in his hand pointed at the stage.

Moore said he then walked to a telephone booth located in a lounge area between the entrance and the auditorium itself, to phone in a story to ABC Radio, for which he was a free-lance reporter. While in the phone booth he saw a man with a .45 caliber automatic in his hand run from the auditorium, through the lounge and past him out the door. He identified the man as the defendant Hayer and said he was the same man he had seen with a gun in the auditorium.

Moore testified that he saw Reuben Francis chasing Hayer, with a revolver in his hand. Francis fired three times, hitting Hayer with the second shot when Hayer was a few feet from the door, Moore claims. Hayer was through the door and out of his line of sight when he heard the third shot, Moore said.

Moore joined the Organization of Afro-American Unity after Malcolm X's death and was appointed chairman in April 1965. He left the organization a few months later, he said.

Detective Joseph Reich, the last of the technical witnesses, testified on February 16 about the results of the ballistics tests he made, involving a variety of bullets, pellets, and shells found at the scene. Reich testified that the four cartridges found in Hayer's pocket when he was arrested had each been in the chamber of the .45 caliber automatic that the prosecution has presented in evidence. This can be determined by "ejector" and "extractor" marks on the shell made when it is removed from the chamber.

Reich testified that he had examined the five .32 caliber bullets recovered but could not tell whether they had been fired from a single gun or as many as five different guns. Three of these bullets were found in the area of the lounge.

One of the .32 caliber bullets was recovered from Hayer's leg March 8, 1965, when he was operated on. No one has explained why the bullet was left in Hayer's leg for more than two weeks.

The last of these bullets was removed from the liver of William Harris on February 22, 1965. According to a police interview with him February 22, 1965, read at the trial, Harris was shot in the right side from behind when he was running out of the ballroom. He told a policeman outside that he had been shot and he was taken to a hospital. The report identified Harris as fifty-one years old and a member of the Organization of Afro-American Unity.

According to another report read at the trial, William Parker, thirty-six, who was seated in the third row on the left side of the audience, was hit in the foot by a pellet, presumably from a shotgun, when the shooting started.

TALMADGE HAYER CONFESSES

New York, March 1—The prosecution's case against two of the three men accused of assassinating Malcolm X was severely shaken February 28 when Talmadge Hayer (also known as Thomas Hagan), the only defendant to have been caught at the scene of the crime, confessed. Hayer not only exonerated Norman 3X Butler and Thomas 15X Johnson, but also described how the crime was committed, and in doing so threw grave doubt on the testimony of most of the prosecution's eyewitnesses.

Vincent Dermody, the assistant district attorney in charge of the case, tried to show that Hayer was lying to save the other two defendants.

Hayer said he had come forward to testify as a witness for the defense and to confess because he wanted the truth to be known: that Butler and Johnson did not have anything to do with the crime. He had not come forward sooner because he didn't want to confess, and had waited until it was clear he needed to in order to prevent the conviction of the two innocent men.

Hayer maintained that he was not and had never been one of Elijah Muhammad's followers—nor were his accomplices, to his knowledge. None of them had any personal motive for killing Malcolm X, but they had been hired to carry out the assassination. He refused to say how much money he had been offered. He said that the man who hired him was not a Muslim either.

Hayer refused to identify his accomplices or the one who hired them. He did drop one hint about who the latter was. In response to a question by Dermody about the identity of the man who offered him money, he said it probably would have been revealed if Williams had been successful in "continuing his interrogation." Williams is one of Butler's lawyers who has cross-examined only a few of the prosecution witnesses. Dermody asked no questions to try to find out from whom Williams could have gotten this information.

Hayer's description of how the assassination took place is much more credible than the story the prosecution said it would prove. It contradicts the prosecution's version in ways from which neither Hayer nor the other defendants benefit, and in ways which make much more sense than the prosecution's version. When Dermody asked Hayer if the witnesses told the truth about him, he responded at one point: "It's quite impossible for the crime to have been committed the way they said it had."

Hayer said that only one man, not two, had been involved in a diversion just before the shooting, and that it had not been himself, as the prosecution alleged. He and another accomplice had taken seats together in the front row on the left side of the auditorium. A man with a shotgun sat in the fourth row. Hayer admitted he had come armed with a .45 caliber automatic and had shot about four times at the prone body of Malcolm X, after Malcolm had been felled by the shotgun blast. His companion had fired at Malcolm with a Luger.

Hayer testified he knew the man with the shotgun for about one year at the time they participated in the assassination. He said the man was dark skinned, very husky, and had a beard. Johnson, who has been accused of firing the shotgun, has a very light complexion. Hayer explained he was willing to describe the man because he had already been described by an earlier defense witness.

Ernest Greene, a twenty-one-year-old former Muslim, had appeared as Butler's eyewitness on February 24, and testified to seeing a stout, dark, bearded man shoot Malcolm X with a shotgun.

Dermody recalled the testimony of the first secret witness from whose testimony reporters had been barred. The secret witness had testified that Butler had been involved in a scuffle near the stairway that leads from the entrance of the ballroom down to the entrance of the building. The witness claimed to have knocked Butler down the stairs and said that Hayer had jumped over Butler on the way out.

Hayer denied seeing any scuffling near the stairs or seeing anyone knocked down the stairs. "I was shot. I didn't do any jumping," he said. When asked about it again, he said: "I couldn't jump over anybody." Hayer was shot in the leg.

In his cross-examination of Hayer, Dermody harped on the fact that Hayer had lied when he testified in his own behalf on February 23 and denied having any part in the crime. He also tried to show that Hayer was a Muslim. This is an important point in the case, for if Hayer is not a Muslim there is every reason to believe he told the truth in his confession, and that the Muslims were not involved in the assassination.

The question raised by Hayer's confession is: Who paid for the murder of Malcolm X? While it is generally assumed that Elijah Muhammad's organization wanted Malcolm out of the way, it should be borne in mind that those who profited the most from his revolutionary voice being silenced are the ruling class of this country.

Dermody has not proved so far that Hayer was a Muslim. Cary Thomas, the first eyewitness, claimed to know that Hayer was a member of the Jersey City mosque, though he testified he'd never been to that mosque. Vernal Temple, the second eyewitness, claimed to have seen Hayer function as a guard in the Harlem mosque and strike someone, who was causing a disturbance, a karate blow on that occasion.

Now Dermody is trying to show that Hayer was a member of the Newark mosque. Dermody has produced two photographs of groups in karate garb, apparently including Hayer. Franklin X Durant testified February 24 that he, a member of Mosque No. 25 in Newark, had taken the photos at a bazaar held in the mosque during the spring of 1963. He identified Hayer in the photos and said Hayer introduced himself as Talmadge, but went on to testify that Hayer was not a member of the mosque. He said most of the others in the photos were not Muslims to his knowledge. Durant said he never saw Hayer in the mosque on any occasion after that. Reportedly, the karate exhibition was put on by a karate school in Newark, but this was never brought out in the testimony.

A number of other witnesses have testified for Butler. Gloria 11X Wills and Juanita 8X Gibbs said they spoke to Butler at his home on the telephone just after the assassination, between 3:05 and 3:30 p.m. Dr. Kenneth Seslowe testified to treating Butler for an infection of the veins in his right leg on the morning of the assassination.

SUMMARY OF THE TESTIMONY

New York, March 8—Testimony in the trial of the three men accused of assassinating Malcolm X ended March 4. On March 7 the defense attorneys summed up the case for each of their clients. Assistant District Attorney Vincent Dermody took all of today's court session to argue the case of the prosecution. All that remains before the jury is sent out tomorrow is Judge Charles Marks's charge to the jury.

At the opening of the prosecution's case on January 21 Dermody summarized what he expected to prove in the trial. He has stuck to that story through thick and thin—despite the fact that one of the defendants made a surprise confession which gave a very different account of what happened.

The evidence that Hayer was one of the assassins is overwhelming. Not only was he shot and caught at the scene of the assassination and identified by many, but before the end of the defense presentation he withdrew his claim of innocence and took the stand to confess.

Even without his confession, the evidence against him was strong. The fact that police testified that he had a clip of .45 caliber bullets in his pocket when he was arrested, and that his thumb print was found on a crude smoke device set off at the rear of the Audubon

Ballroom at the time of the shooting, would have dispelled any lingering doubts in the minds of the jurors.

The prosecution presented ten eyewitnesses altogether who claimed to have seen at least one of the defendants at the scene of the crime. Three of them identified only Hayer, and five others identified Hayer and at least one other defendant. Altogether, four identified Johnson, and two of them claimed to see a shotgun in his hand. Six identified Butler, and three of them said he had a pistol.

No material evidence was presented linking Butler or Johnson to the crime or even demonstrating that they were present at the Audubon Ballroom when Malcolm X was gunned down. The evidence against them was the testimony of the eyewitnesses.

Both Butler and Johnson were and are active Muslims who were well known to a number of Malcolm X's followers and guards. Malcolm X had charged that followers of Elijah Muhammad had tried to attack him several times. His followers were watching for and would most likely have noticed Muslims like Butler and Johnson. On the face of it, it is unlikely that Butler and Johnson would have entered the ballroom where Malcolm X was holding a meeting and not have been noticed. Eyewitness testimony against them would have to be solid and reliable to be believed.

Cary Thomas, the first eyewitness, claimed to have seen all three participating in the assassination or holding a gun, but the inconsistencies in his story were so great as to call his testimony into question. His testimony before the grand jury last March was very different from the story he told in court.

Though he claimed to have been a follower of Elijah Muhammad and then of Malcolm X, by his own testimony Thomas didn't behave like a Muslim or understand anything about what Malcolm X stood for. He was placed in Bellevue Hospital for psychiatric examination in 1963, screaming, "I did not kill Jesus Christ." His condition was diagnosed as psychoneurosis.

Thomas was picked up by the police for questioning on March 2, 1965, and held as a material witness. While he was being held he was charged with burning a mattress, and indicted for arson. He was transferred to a regular prison, and has been held on this charge since then.

Charles Blackwell, the ninth eyewitness, was the only other one to identify all three defendants. He too told a completely different story to the grand jury, but he testified that he lied before the grand jury rather than in the court. His courtroom story corresponded with what the prosecution said it would prove, as did Cary Thomas's courtroom version.

Blackwell was the guard at the front of the stage on the left side, where the shooting took place. According to his courtroom testimony, Butler and Hayer ran by him to the stage where they shot Malcolm X. After they turned around and began running out, he "gave chase." It was at this point, incredibly enough, that he noticed a man "standing four or five rows back" who looked "startled" or "scared." Blackwell identified this man as Johnson, but he said he saw no gun in his hand. He claimed to have seen Johnson then run into the ladies' lounge.

The two other witnesses who identified Johnson are Vernal Temple, the second eyewitness, and Fred Williams, the eighth. Temple claimed to have recognized Johnson, whom he knew only as "15X," sitting at the back of the auditorium when he entered. He said the only time he had ever seen Johnson before that was at a Muslim convention in Chicago in 1962. He had a notoriously bad memory about everything else connected with that convention, and contradicted himself a number of times.

Williams said he saw Johnson holding a shotgun. He also claimed to recognize Butler as one of the two men involved in a scuffle which preceded the shooting and served as a diversion. He saw no gun in Butler's hand, he said. Williams was a friend of Blackwell's at the time and drove Blackwell to the Audubon Ballroom that day. His memory was very foggy about nearly everything but the events in the Audubon.

The fifth witness, Jasper Davis, identified only Butler. He said that Butler sat down next to him and they struck up a conversation. Then another man walked down the aisle and Butler called to him.

That man sat next to Butler. The disturbance that preceded the shooting was created by these two men, Davis testified, though he was not sure which one of them did the shouting. Davis didn't notice either of them fire a gun, he said.

Davis picked Butler out of a police lineup of eight men. None of the others in the lineup fitted the description he had given the police of the man involved, Davis testified—though the description he gave was very general. Much of the identification of Butler centered around a gray tweed coat he was allegedly wearing. Only one other man in the lineup wore a gray coat, said Davis, and it was not similar to the one Butler was wearing.

Edward DiPina, the third eyewitness, said he saw both Butler and Hayer shoot at the stage from where they stood up in the third row in the audience, and then turn around and run out. Cross-examination proved DiPina to be a very confused—if not senile—old man. For example, DiPina identified one of the defense attorneys as the detective who drove him to Bellevue Hospital to identify Hayer.

The seventh eyewitness, Ronald Timberlake, testified in secret—reporters and spectators were barred from the courtroom. But much of his testimony has since been made known. He claimed to have knocked Butler down the stairs that lead from the auditorium to the entrance of the building. The crowd then held and pummeled Butler but he managed to get away. The witness claimed that Hayer, who had been shot in the leg by this time, jumped over Butler on his way down the stairs.

The secret witness also testified that he retrieved a .45 caliber automatic on the stairs which he turned over to an FBI agent. That agent also testified secretly. This is the .45 that has been placed in evidence, and is allegedly the weapon that Hayer used.

The reason for this dubious tale about knocking Butler down the stairs became clear when the prosecution introduced in evidence a photo of Butler taken on February 26, 1965, soon after he was arrested. It showed that Butler had a swollen ankle and both legs were discolored.

This photo was introduced during the cross-examination of one of Butler's defense witnesses, Dr. Kenneth Seslowe of Jacobi Hospital. Dr. Seslowe testified that Butler had been treated at the hospital by another doctor on January 22, 1965, for infected wounds of both shins. He himself had treated Butler on the morning of February 21, 1965, the day of the assassination. Butler complained of pain in the right leg, and the illness was diagnosed as superficial thrombophlebitis. Butler's leg was bandaged; he was given oral medication; and he was told to stay off his feet, keep his leg elevated, and apply hot soaks to it.

Butler also had three witnesses who testified he was at home at the time of or shortly after the shooting. Butler's wife Theresa said he returned home about 12:55 p.m. and never left the house that day. Two sisters of Mosque No. 7, to which the Butlers belong, testified they telephoned and spoke with Butler between 3:05 and 3:30 p.m. shortly after hearing of the shooting on the radio.

Johnson's wife testified he was home all day on February 21, 1965. One of his neighbors, Edward Long, a Muslim, testified he visited Johnson at his home between 3:30 and 4:30 that day. Malcolm X is said to have been shot at about 3:05 or 3:10.

Two eyewitnesses testified for the defense. Ernest Greene, twenty-one, a former Muslim, testified he saw the man who shot Malcolm X with a shotgun and described him as very stout, very dark, and wearing a heavy beard. He said it was not Johnson, who is very light skinned and wore no beard.

The most spectacular eyewitness was Talmadge Hayer, who confessed in order to testify that Butler and Johnson had nothing to do with the crime. He maintained that he and his accomplices were not Muslims but were hired killers. Hayer's confession was quite convincing, but the prosecution refused to believe him.

One of the most convincing things about Hayer's confession is that his account of how the crime was committed is plausible and corresponds to eyewitness accounts of the events that were never brought out in the trial. For example, Hayer testified that he and his accomplice, who both had pistols, sat in the first row; the man with the shotgun sat in the fourth row; and the accomplice who created the diversion by standing and yelling sat somewhere behind the man with the shotgun.

According to an eyewitness account in the *Baltimore Afro-American* of February 27, 1965, two or three men with guns rose from the first row, while those that created the disturbance took no part in the shooting. It is unlikely that the same men who were going to shoot Malcolm X first stood up and yelled to call attention to themselves.

Dermody still insists that Hayer is a Muslim trying to protect his alleged accomplices. But Dermody has not come close to proving that Hayer is a Muslim. Vernal Temple claimed to have seen Hayer in Mosque No. 7 in Harlem once in the summer of 1964, functioning as a guard and wearing a white armband with red letters "Muhammad." But he also testified that he stopped attending meetings in the mosque after Malcolm X was suspended—which was in late November 1963. Besides, according to testimony at the trial, armbands were never worn in the mosque but were worn at a convention in Chicago. It is hard to believe that the prosecution would be reduced to such flimsy testimony as the major evidence of Hayer's being a Muslim if he really were.

In my opinion the weight of evidence points to the conclusion that Johnson and Butler had nothing to do with the assassination and were not even at the Audubon Ballroom that day. It would be a monstrous miscarriage of justice if they are found "guilty beyond a reasonable doubt."

MYSTERY NOT SOLVED BY VERDICT

New York—On March 11, after twenty hours of deliberation, the jury in the Malcolm X murder trial returned a verdict of guilty against all three defendants: Talmadge Hayer (also known as Thomas Hagan), Norman 3X Butler, and Thomas 15X Johnson. Sentencing will take place on April 14.

The jury was presented with two accounts of the assassination. Assistant District Attorney Dermody claimed that the three defendants, all active members of the Nation of Islam, did the shooting according to a prearranged plan: Butler and Hayer created a diversion in a middle row of the auditorium, whereupon Johnson ran to the stage and shot Malcolm X with a sawed-off shotgun. Then Hayer and Butler ran to the stage and fired pistol shots into the prone body.

The New York police decided that the Muslims had committed the crime right after the assassination. The police made statements to the press that Hayer was a Muslim and they sought his accomplices among the Muslims. The police and district attorney's office stuck to that story and avoided looking elsewhere for the killers. The other version of the assassination was given by Hayer when he took the stand for a second time and confessed to being one of the assassins. He said he had been hired to do the killing, as had his three accomplices, but that none of the gunmen nor the man who hired them was a Muslim. Butler and Johnson were in no way involved, he said. Hayer's account of what happened in the ballroom was much more convincing than Dermody's, and squared with eyewitness accounts in the press at the time: Hayer and an accomplice sat in the first row with pistols. Another man sat in the fourth row with a sawed-off shotgun. A fourth man sat further back and created the disturbance, but he was not involved in the shooting.

The outcome of the trial depended on which of these two stories the jury thought was essentially correct. Dermody stuck to this issue—hammering away at Hayer's confession, insisting that it was a lie and that Hayer was a Muslim out to save his fellow Muslims.

The defense attorneys largely ignored the real issue and concocted instead a fantastic theory that Malcolm was assassinated by a conspiracy of his more politically oriented followers, who framed the defendants. Dermody had no difficulty in smashing this theory.

I have no special knowledge about whether or not Hayer was a Muslim. But it is clear that the prosecution never established that he was. Yet the defense did not hammer at that fact sufficiently to make it clear in the minds of the jurors. If Hayer was not a Muslim, there was no reason to believe Dermody's contention that Hayer's confession was a trick to save his Muslim brothers.

The defense was inadequate in other ways as well. All four of the lawyers for Butler and Johnson were court appointed. Though they are all Negroes, and apparently sympathetic to the defendants, they were unwilling or unable to do a thorough job.

The defense attorneys always took for granted the integrity of the police and prosecution. They didn't point out to the jury how the police operate in selecting out malleable witnesses and rehearsing their testimony until they remember what they're supposed to. The defense attorneys were willing to rock the boat just a little but not enough to even raise the possibility of turning it over. They mentioned some of the contradictions in the testimony of the prosecution witnesses, but omitted most of them and never hammered at the pattern of contradictions enough to ensure that the jurors understood that the witnesses were lying or unreliable.

In a French film about a murder trial I once saw, besides the prosecutor who represented the state and the attorney who represented the defendant, there was a third attorney who represented the slain man. That third point of view was what was lacking at this trial. For neither the prosecution nor the defense attorneys were interested in finding the truth about the assassination.

For example, Reuben Francis is a key person whose testimony was necessary in order to find out what happened that day. Witnesses claimed that he had shot Hayer, that he was in charge of organizing protection for Malcolm X, and that he had been given two of the murder weapons found in the ballroom—one of which disappeared. Francis is in prison on the charge of shooting Hayer, and available to both sides, yet he was not called to testify.

A great many other people who could have helped establish the truth about the assassination never were called. A number of eyewitness accounts of the assassination appeared in the press, but the reporters were not subpoenaed to testify.

The only major fact established at the trial is that Hayer was one of the assassins. Most probably he and his accomplices were hired killers.

All the important questions surrounding the assassination still remain to be answered:

Who ordered the assassination? Those who had a motive include Elijah Muhammad and his followers, right-wing and racist organizations, the U.S. government, and private agencies of the American ruling class.

What role did the New York police play in the assassination? Why didn't they provide at least their usual protection accorded Malcolm X's meetings regularly? Just a week before an attempt had been made on Malcolm's life in which his home was burned down.

Did the police knowingly protect one of the people involved in the killing who was caught by the crowd? Reliable press reports stated that the police rescued two suspects from the audience, and the matter has still not been clarified. Was the man a police agent?

Were any of the witnesses at the trial police agents or police informers? It is very likely that such agents were present at the assassination, but none came forward to testify.

All these questions remain, but the police have no desire to pursue them. It is quite possible that the final responsibility for the assassination rests with those who run this country, and that the police were involved at least to the extent of being kept from interfering with the crime and from hunting for the real killers.

4

Myths about Malcolm X

by George Breitman

This talk was given at the Friday Night Socialist Forum in Detroit on March 17, 1967, in response to a speech at the same forum by Reverend Albert B. Cleage, then the chairman of the Detroit Inner City Organizing Committee, on February 24, 1967. The texts of both speeches were first printed in International Socialist Review, September–October 1967, under the title "Myths About Malcolm X: Two Views."

Three weeks ago the Friday Night Socialist Forum held its third memorial meeting for one of the greatest men of our time, Malcolm X. It was organized in such a way as to provide a broad range of opinion. There was a panel of several local poets, headed by Dudley Randall, reading their contributions to the new book, *For Malcolm: Poems on the Life and the Death of Malcolm X*. The chairman was attorney Milton Henry, who had worked with Malcolm, published the magnificent record of Malcolm's "Message to the Grass Roots," and was the principal speaker at our second memorial meeting one year ago. The speakers were Dave Wesley of SNCC, Derrick Morrison of the Young Socialist Alliance, and Reverend Albert Cleage, chairman of the Inner City Organizing Committee.

The usual custom at the Friday Night Socialist Forum is to have a discussion period after the formal talks, with the audience invited to ask questions or express opinions. But it was not considered proper to have a discussion period at a memorial meeting, and it was omitted three weeks ago. However, there was an unusual amount of desire for further discussion expressed after that meeting, much of it stimulated by the remarks of Reverend Cleage. And so the committee in charge of the forum decided to have another meeting on the subject at the first open date, which was tonight, and to follow the customary practice allowing for discussion.

Much of what Reverend Cleage dealt with in his talk concerned myths about Malcolm X, or what he considered to be myths. I am going to deal with the same subject—myths about Malcolm X, or what I consider to be myths. Since I have spoken and written about this subject before and it is a vast subject, I shall try to confine myself tonight mainly to points raised by Reverend Cleage. That is, I will take his remarks as a point of departure for mine.

Someone asked me if I think it worthwhile to give a whole talk in that form. My answer, of course, is yes. In *The Last Year of Malcolm X*, I spent a whole chapter discussing the interpretations of Malcolm made by Bayard Rustin, the social-democratic reformist and pacifist, and I consider Reverend Cleage to be a much more important figure in the movement than Bayard Rustin. In 1964, for example, Reverend Cleage led the most advanced expression of independent black political action in the country—the Freedom Now Party—at a time when Bayard Rustin was campaigning for Johnson and pressuring the Mississippi Freedom Democratic Party to accept Johnson's rotten compromise offer at the Atlantic City convention of the Democratic Party. It is true that two years later Reverend Cleage took a backward step—a very wrong and harmful step, in our opinion—when he went back into the Democratic Party to run as a Democratic candidate in a primary election. But even so, he remains the spokesman for an important, militant wing of the black freedom movement, and a leader and sponsor of campaigns worthy of support, which we have supported despite his backward step; and what he said in his talk three weeks ago, which I think was his first on the subject of Malcolm X, deserves serious consideration.

[The next portion, a 10-minute summary of Reverend Cleage's speech, is omitted from this transcription.]*

That ends my summary of Reverend Cleage's speech. Of course I haven't done it justice as rhetoric; Reverend Cleage is one of the best orators in the country, one of the few people who could speak from the same platform as Malcolm without looking bad by comparison. But I have presented all of his main ideas, points, and implications as objectively as I could.

I agree with Reverend Cleage that there has been a profusion of myths spread about Malcolm in the two years since his death, and in a moment I will try to explain why. But I don't agree with him when he says there is a danger that the real Malcolm will be forgotten or obscured through distortion. There was a danger of that when Malcolm was killed, but I don't think it is a serious danger any longer; at any rate, the danger has grown smaller. I don't think the real Malcolm can successfully be distorted—whatever Reverend Cleage may say, whatever I may say, and no matter how many more myths may be manufactured and circulated. Because the truth is now too widely known, and becoming better known every day—the whole truth, and not just part of it.

When Malcolm died, there was virtually nothing of what he had said in print. But since then many thousands of people have had the chance to read and hear what Malcolm said, including large numbers who had never heard of Malcolm while he was alive. Milton Henry told me three weeks ago that he had just returned from the West Coast, where he had spoken at a memorial celebration for

---

* It was omitted because Breitman's speech was originally printed together with the full text of Cleage's speech. Although the omitted portion is not available now, Reverend Cleage's main arguments are restated later by Breitman.—Ed.

Malcolm (there were more such memorials held this year than in the previous two), and he said he had run into children, literally children, who were quoting passages from *Malcolm X Speaks*. And they were quoting what Malcolm really said and thought, not myths. So we have to keep on knocking down any and all myths that are raised, but I believe we can do this in a spirit of optimism, not despair, because the truth is on the march.

There are many reasons for the myths. Malcolm was a remarkable man, a great man, and when he died, he became a folk hero. Even if we leave aside the unsolved questions about who arranged the assassination, which were bound to spur various speculations and rumors, Malcolm was the kind of man around whom legends grow—not necessarily hostile legends, either; favorable ones too.

But there are other reasons for misconceptions about Malcolm. One of these was the fact that Malcolm was cut down before he had finished his work, before he had formulated all of his ideas and brought them together in a consistent whole. In his last year many people thought or knew that Malcolm was developing new ideas, perhaps a new body of thought, theory, or philosophy. But because of the press distortions, and because Malcolm did not yet have an organization capable of reaching the masses, they didn't know exactly or fully what his thinking was after he left the Black Muslims. This is always a breeding ground for rumor and myth.

More than that. One of the things that distinguished Malcolm from almost all of his contemporaries was his ability to grow, to change, to move forward; even—how hard this is!—to admit an error and correct it. These qualities became more prominent after he broke away from the dogmas of Elijah Muhammad and began, as he put it, to think for himself. Free to think for himself and to speak for himself, he had the courage to admit to himself he had been wrong about something if he thought that was so, and the courage to admit it publicly, and to present a new position that he thought was more correct than an old one. It is the rareness of this quality, along with the vital importance of the questions he was reconsidering, that makes a study of his evolution during his last year so rewarding.

But to people whose minds are fixed in a rut—that is, most of us—this was confusing. It wasn't that Malcolm was confused, but that some people, whose impressions of Malcolm had been formed and hardened and pigeonholed when he was a Black Muslim, some of these people became confused when Malcolm changed a position during his last year—merely because he wasn't saying word for word and slogan for slogan what they had become accustomed to hearing him say. No matter how logically, how lucidly Malcolm stated these new positions, such people remained confused—some to this day; and when they spoke, their confusion contributed to myths about Malcolm.

And finally there was the malicious motivation for myths, which Reverend Cleage referred to. Because Malcolm became a martyr and hero after his death, some groups have tried to claim him for their own, even though they did not speak up for him when he was alive. They have tried to "interpret" him in such a way as to make his views appear to coincide with their own. In order to do this, they have to try to make us forget embarrassing facts such as their dislike of some of the positions he took.

So what they do is chop Malcolm up, keeping the parts they like, the parts it suits their purposes to remember, and discarding the other parts as unimportant or irrelevant where they don't deny their existence altogether. This attempt to preserve only part of Malcolm, the part they find useful, while ignoring or denying the other parts that are needed if you want to see the real Malcolm, the whole Malcolm, is of course bound to result in myths, even if they are presented in the name of opposing myths.

Reverend Cleage is absolutely correct when he labels as a myth the story that Malcolm became an "integrationist" as a result of his trip to Mecca in the spring of 1964. This myth, or lie, is spread, as you can expect, by integrationists. Malcolm did not become an "integrationist" at Mecca, or at any time after that. Until the day of his death he remained an opponent of what is generally or popularly understood, or misunderstood, as "integration." I find it easy to join Reverend Cleage on this point because we, the Marxists, have been exposing and opposing the myth since Malcolm died, even though Reverend Cleage's remarks may have left some ambiguity about this.

But while Malcolm did not become an "integrationist" at Mecca, or after, his views on race did begin to change at Mecca—his views on race, race relations, black-white relations, the possibility of eventual brotherhood. They began to change there, and they changed even more after he left Mecca and went to Africa and held discussions with many revolutionary Africans. Reverend Cleage did not mention this, but the impact of revolutionary African thinking on Malcolm was much greater and deeper and more profound than the impact of Mecca.

The change, stated too briefly, was this: Not that Malcolm embraced "integration" as a solution, but that he saw the cause of racial oppression in a new light. He saw it as rooted not merely in racial or color differences, but in economic, political, social, and cultural exploitation. From this he began to conclude not that "integration" is the answer, but that racial conflict might be eliminated by eliminating exploitation; that racial enmity is not inherent in human beings or immutable or necessarily ordained to last for all time; and that it is possible (not certain) that eventually, someday (not now) oppressed blacks and oppressed whites might be able to march together in genuine brotherhood and fight together against their common oppressors and exploiters. But, and he always qualified this thought immediately, it can't happen until the blacks first organize themselves independently and create their own movement, their own power. No worthwhile alliance can be created, he insisted, until blacks come together first and create their own organization with their own uncompromising program.

Now Reverend Cleage says he doesn't believe what Malcolm is supposed to have said at Mecca; he says Malcolm wouldn't have been taken in by the window dressing, that Malcolm was too intelligent to believe that blacks and whites could march together, and so on. Well, this is really an argument between Reverend Cleage and Malcolm, not between Reverend Cleage and people who accurately report what Malcolm said and wrote. Perhaps Reverend Cleage believes that Malcolm was not saying what he really thought; if he does, he should explain why. I, for one, after carefully studying everything I could find, believe that Malcolm said what he thought, popular or unpopular, especially after he left the Black Muslims, was no longer under their discipline and no longer required to express their ideas. If Reverend Cleage believes that what Malcolm said and wrote has been misrepresented by others, then I think he has the obligation to examine what Malcolm said (available on many tapes) and what he wrote (available in his own handwriting) and to show where the reports are inaccurate or misleading.

It is not enough to say merely, "I don't believe it." It is necessary in addition to square this disbelief with the evidence of Malcolm's own voice and Malcolm's own pen, and show why that evidence cannot be accepted or trusted. Reverend Cleage said that what has happened with Malcolm enables him to understand better the various myths about Jesus. But we have nothing about Jesus now except myths; we've got facts about Malcolm to balance along with myths. The world has changed since the time of Jesus, and in some ways it has changed for the better—especially technologically. I am thinking about the discovery and development of the tape recorder—a marvelous invention. Thanks to it, we can hear and know what Malcolm said, which is the best antidote to mythology that I can imagine.

So Reverend Cleage is on firm ground in rejecting the myth that Malcolm became an "integrationist." But the reasons he gives for rejecting it are not so sound, and the conclusions he tries to draw—that Malcolm did not change *any* of his views—have not been demonstrated factually or logically; and I don't think they can be demonstrated.

I cannot go along with Reverend Cleage when he says that it is a myth that Malcolm wanted to internationalize the Afro-American struggle. Malcolm spoke here in Detroit twice after leaving the Black Muslims—in April 1964, and in February 1965, one week before his death. On both these occasions Reverend Cleage was present, and at both of them Malcolm called for internationalizing the struggle. What he said both times is preserved on tape, as are many other speeches when he said the same thing. So this is a matter of fact, easily verified.

Besides the question of the fact there is the question of interpreting the fact. Reverend Cleage spoke of people who have a mystique about Africa and who say that Malcolm said that the African nations are going to free American black people, and therefore all that Afro-Americans have to do is sit around and wait for that happy day. I haven't run into many people with this particular interpretation of Malcolm's call to internationalize the struggle, but of course Reverend Cleage is correct to pronounce this as a distortion and myth, which can only do harm by promoting passivity instead of struggle.

But this particular distortion or misunderstanding of what Malcolm was talking about does not change the fact that Malcolm did advocate an alliance of Afro-Americans with Africans and other nonwhites to coordinate their struggles, and even their strategy, against their common enemy, against what Malcolm called "the international power structure," whose headquarters he correctly placed in Washington, D.C. I don't see how anybody can question the fact that Malcolm became an internationalist (this is one of the things that made him so dangerous in the eyes of the imperialists and their CIA), and that internationalism, by definition, means efforts to internationalize the struggle.

One of the ways in which Malcolm sought to internationalize the struggle was by bringing an indictment of racism against the United States government before the United Nations, a "world court." He raised this proposal immediately after he left the Black Muslims in the spring of 1964, and he worked hard trying to get African leaders to bring the indictment into the United Nations, and to get American civil rights leaders to join in promoting this project. He did not succeed, for various reasons, but he still had it on his agenda at his death.

When he first publicly raised this project in the spring of 1964, he tended to overstate its possibilities—that is, he gave too rosy a picture of what the probable results would be. The *Militant* printed an article by me in May 1964, supporting Malcolm's proposal to take Washington to the United Nations and expose its racism and hypocrisy, but noting that the U.S. government and its allies control the United Nations, and that the UN cannot be expected to do anything seriously against the interests of American imperialism. I didn't say it as pungently as Reverend Cleage did three weeks ago, when he said you can't expect any more justice from the so-called world court than you can from the Supreme Court or Detroit's Recorder's Court, because all of them are run by crackers, but I said essentially the same thing almost three years ago. Even though my article was critical, Malcolm sent me a message of thanks for writing it.

Now Reverend Cleage says Malcolm *couldn't* have believed that much would be accomplished by going to the United Nations, and therefore it is a myth to say he wanted to internationalize the struggle. But this is a fallacy of oversimplification, and a non sequitur. The truth is more complex, and the conclusion to be drawn different. Malcolm *did* get carried away at the beginning about the possibilities of taking Washington to the UN; I am sorry to say this now, as I was sorry to say it then, but it happens to be the truth. And the truth is what we are after, not simplifications. So: at the beginning Malcolm went overboard in what he said could be accomplished by going to the UN. Later, however, he took a more balanced view of the project, he stopped speaking of it as a move that could solve the problems of black people, he corrected himself in assessing its probable results. But he continued to push this project. After modifying what he said about it, he continued to work for it. Because he did want to internationalize the struggle—that's no myth—and this was one way of doing it, even though it would not be the final solution, but only a step in that direction. If Malcolm was ready to acknowledge and correct mistakes, I don't think we do him or the struggle any service by denying either the mistake or the correction; or by saying "I don't believe" he made this mistake in order to deny that he wanted to internationalize the struggle.

Reverend Cleage's stated intention—to explode myths in order to preserve the real Malcolm—can only be applauded. But I am afraid that he was only partly successful with some of the myths he aimed at, and that in the process he may have contributed some myths of his own.

His basic mistake, I think, is to present Malcolm the Black Muslim as the real Malcolm, the only one worth remembering, the only one worth building on and continuing from—and to dismiss as unimportant, inconsistent, or irrelevant the last year of Malcolm's life, when Malcolm himself began to build on and continue from his previous positions. This, I submit, is not the way to see or understand the whole Malcolm. Reverend Cleage mentioned the blind men, each of whom touched a different part of the elephant and came up with a different concept of the elephant. Reverend Cleage is doing that too—he's saying the hide is the elephant, and the feet and the tail—but not the trunk or the tusks. It is harder to forgive him than those blind men, because he is not blind, and all the parts of Malcolm can be easily seen by anyone who wants to look at them.

I say Malcolm is both the Malcolm of the period before the split and the Malcolm of the year after the split, and I want to see and understand the whole man. I want to see the whole man—the parts that remained constant and never changed, and the parts that did not remain constant and did change; the parts that fit preconceived notions and the parts that contradict preconceived notions; what he was trying to do after he decided to think for himself instead of with the mind of Elijah Muhammad; and in what direction he was moving. That is why in editing his speeches, I included everything available, not just the parts I agree with. That is why in the book about his evolution I was just as concerned with presenting his positions that diverge from my own as I was with exploring those that resemble or approach mine. If I didn't do that, I wouldn't really have the right to talk about myths spread by other people. A myth can consist of nothing but the exclusion of relevant facts.

Reverend Cleage wants, in effect, to dismiss the last year of Malcolm's life; he could find only one favorable statement to make about that year—that Malcolm was beginning to make a transition to organization, to structure. The last year was the period when Malcolm was developing his own ideas rather than popularizing those of Elijah Muhammad. The reason Reverend Cleage wants to dismiss the last year is not that he agrees with all of the ideas of Elijah Muhammad, but that he disagrees with some of the ideas Malcolm was expressing in this, the independent phase of his life. In a moment I will list some of those ideas. First, I want to call your attention to the way that Reverend Cleage seeks to justify such dismissal.

In the last year, Reverend Cleage says, Malcolm was under constant harassment, under fierce pressure, under never-ending threat of assassination. All of this is completely true. As a result, Reverend Cleage continues, Malcolm made a number of confused and confusing statements, fragmentary statements, which unscrupulous people use to distort the meaning and tradition of Malcolm. Is *that* true?—not that Malcolm's statements are used or misused, but is it true that Malcolm's last year was distinguished by confused and confusing statements?

Reverend Cleage says it is true, I say it is not true, and it is up to you to find the answer. Because on it will depend your judgement about whether the real Malcolm tradition ended when he left the Black Muslims, or whether it continued and reached a higher level after he left.

How are you going to decide this? Reverend Cleage more or less invites you to take his word for it, since he doesn't suggest any alternative or offer any documentation or evidence. I invite you not to take my word, because there is an alternative. And that is: Read what Malcolm said during his last year. Read it for yourself and judge for yourself if it is confused or confusing—or just the opposite.

Read the book *Malcolm X Speaks,* which contains everything from his last year that was available at the time it was published at the end of 1965. It has been in print now for one and a half years and has now been read by tens of thousands of people. So far, not one challenge to its veracity or accuracy has been publicly presented by anybody. *Liberator,* a magazine which is not sympathetic with the views of the editor of *Malcolm X Speaks,* calls it "the source book for what Malcolm actually said."

Then, after you have read it, if you have the slightest doubt about its accuracy, you should listen to the tapes from which most of *Malcolm X Speaks* was taken. I have listed them all at the end of *The Last Year*—twenty-two tapes from Malcolm's last year—which are available for anyone who wants to listen to them. And since *The Last Year* was printed there are three more tapes from that period that have become available.

By this method, I contend, you can arrive at a solid judgment not only about the accuracy of the printed material by Malcolm, but also about whether the ideas presented there are confused or confusing; and about whether they are fragmentary, that is, presented out of context. I have no doubt whatever that the outcome of this method of investigation will establish conclusively that it is a myth to assert that Malcolm's statements in his last year were anything but lucid, carefully thought out, closely argued, and amazingly consistent, despite all the adverse conditions under which he had to operate.

Now what were some of the main ideas that Malcolm developed and adopted in his last year? I cannot deal with this fully tonight, but I have tried to do it in *The Last Year of Malcolm X.* There I have presented Malcolm's main ideas, citing in each case the source, the place, the date, etc., and including both the ideas I agree with and the ones I question or differ with. In addition, I have given my interpretation, *my* interpretation of the significance, trend, and direction of these ideas. It will not surprise me if some people will disagree with my interpretations, but it will surprise me if anyone successfully challenges the facts I have presented there.

Malcolm came to the conclusion that the Black Muslims had gone as far as they could go, and he wanted to go further. He wanted to get into the active struggle, influence it ideologically, and revolutionize it. He wanted to build a new movement, on new foundations, and therefore he reviewed all his ideas—keeping some, modifying others, casting aside still others. He began to move to the left.

The concept that "the white man is the enemy," which Reverend

Cleage calls the essential strand in Malcolm's philosophy, is the beginning of wisdom for black people who have had illusions that the white power structure is going to hand them freedom on a platter someday. To reject that illusion, and to get to understand that the black man has to fight for freedom, and that he has to depend first of all on his own organized strength, on black power—that is a great step forward, an indispensable step. But it is the beginning of wisdom, not the end of it; it is not a formula sufficient by itself for achieving freedom. After the need for independent black power is learned and absorbed and becomes a guide for action, there are other questions that have to be asked and answered.

If the whites are the enemy, are all whites equally enemies?— both the whites who have the power in this country, the rulers, and the whites who don't have power, and who are exploited by the rulers—not exploited as much as black people, but exploited too? If the whites are the enemy, is there some way of dividing the enemy, splitting them, driving a wedge in among them, setting them to fighting each other—to the benefit of the blacks? If the whites are the enemy, is there some way of transforming the situation so that some of the whites can be demobilized, or neutralized, or even, under certain circumstances, turned into allies or potential allies of the blacks because it would be in their own self-interest?

These are some of the questions Malcolm was beginning to think about and work out in his last year. The main allies of Afro-Americans, he decided, are the black, brown, yellow, and red people of the world; but then he also began to see the possibility of alliances with what he called "militant white" Americans. In fact, he said, to bring about the changes that are needed such alliances will be necessary. He didn't think they would be consummated right away—first, he always stressed, blacks must organize themselves independently, with their own leaders, their own movement, their own program. After they did that, which was his main preoccupation—then there might be alliances with militant whites, the right kind of alliances. And by the right kind of alliances he did not mean working in the Democratic Party.

None of this made him into an "integrationist." But it did make him go beyond the simple formula, the white man is the enemy, which is not the end of wisdom. It did make him think about and study the causes of racism and to see the possibility of its elimination some day. It led him to study the nature of American capitalist society, and of world capitalism—always from the viewpoint of how the interests of black people could be promoted and protected. And from his thought and study—especially from the thinking initiated through his discussions with African revolutionaries (whose impact on him far exceeded the influence of the religious Muslims in Mecca)—he came to the conclusion that capitalism is the cause of racism, that you can't have capitalism without racism, and therefore socialism should seriously be considered as an objective by black Americans as well as by Africans and Asians and Latin Americans. At the very least, you can say that in his last year he became prosocialist and anticapitalist.

Now these are only a few of the ideas Malcolm was thinking about and trying to work out in his last year, and on some of them, I want to be the first to stress, he had not completed his thinking when he was struck down. Reverend Cleage, who doesn't agree with some of these ideas, wants to discard these parts from the Malcolm tradition as irrelevant, as confused. He says the great speech, "Message to the Grass Roots," made while Malcolm was still in the Nation of Islam, is his last will and testament. But I think the evidence shows that Malcolm added to that testament, if you want to call it that, much that is rich, valuable, indispensable, and that he did it knowingly, consciously, and with a clear mind. You may not agree with what he added, but can't say he didn't add it, or that he added it out of confusion.

I would also like to offer an explanation of why Reverend Cleage rejects the contributions of Malcolm's last year. Reverend Cleage is, and has been since the end of 1963, an advocate and defender of black nationalism. Now when I say that, I am not—as anyone who knows me or the Marxist position is aware—I am not attacking him or using the term as an epithet. As I have said and written for many years, black nationalism is progressive and potentially revolutionary. To show what I mean by black nationalism, to show that it is not a negative thing to me, I would like to read you the definition of black nationalism presented in *The Last Year of Malcolm X*. Black nationalism, I say, "is the tendency for black people in the United States to unite as a group, as a people, into a movement of their own to fight for freedom, justice and equality. Animated by the desire of an oppressed minority to decide its own destiny, this tendency holds that black people must control their own movement and the political, economic and social institutions of the black community. Its characteristic attributes include racial pride, group consciousness, hatred of white supremacy, a striving for independence from white control, and identification with black and non-white oppressed groups in other parts of the world." End of definition. In the same chapter I try to show why black nationalism should not be equated with what is called separatism by those who advocate a separate black nation, but I can't go into that here.

If the definition of black nationalism I have just given is correct, then Reverend Cleage is a black nationalist, and that is not an epithet but, from my standpoint, a scientifically correct designation and an expression of respect. Also, according to this definition, Malcolm was a black nationalist, and remained one to his last day—even though in his final months he began to wonder if that was the right label to describe what he was after.

But within the broad category of black nationalism it is possible to see many subdivisions. (This is one of the reasons why the various kinds of black nationalists unfortunately have been unable so far to unite into a single nationwide movement.) For present purposes I cannot discuss the various subdivisions of black nationalism but have to concentrate on the one I call "pure and simple."

In *Marxism and the Negro Struggle*, written in 1964, and again in *The Last Year*, I have presented the argument that "The pure and simple black nationalist is concerned exclusively or primarily with the internal problems of the Negro community, with organizing it, with helping it to gain control of the community's politics, economy, etc. He is not concerned, or is less concerned, with the problems of the total American society, or with the nature of the larger society within which the Negro community exists. He has no theory or program for changing that society; for him that is the white man's problem."

When Reverend Cleage became a black nationalist, he became a pure and simple nationalist (in fact, it was by studying his statements, activities, and development that I first became aware of this subdivision), and he remains a pure and simple nationalist. Malcolm too was a pure and simple nationalist before he left the Black Muslims, and he remained one for the first few months after the split. But then, after his first trip to Africa in the spring of 1964, mainly as a result of the thinking started by his discussions with African revolutionaries, he began to move beyond pure and simple nationalism, to transcend it—if not transcend it, to add something to it that changed it into something else. What was it he added? He added the belief that society as a whole has to be changed, revolutionized, if black people are to achieve their freedom. This did not contradict his conviction that blacks must control their own community, that is, his black nationalism; it was an addition to his black nationalism. Black control of the black community, yes—but that is not enough, because even a black-controlled black community inside a reactionary and exploitative social and economic and political system cannot provide full and genuine freedom. The implication is that Afro-Americans must fight not only to gain control of their community but also to change society as a whole, to reconstruct it on a truly nonexploitative basis.

Malcolm accepted this implication, which is profoundly revolutionary, without ceasing to be a black nationalist. Reverend Cleage does not accept this implication. That, I believe, is the theoretical explanation for Reverend Cleage's tendency to reject most of Malcolm's last period, and, perhaps, not even study it with the care it deserves.

This is not only a mistake, but a sad mistake because Malcolm was ready to give his life, he did give his life, for the right to be able to say the things he did in his last year. I mean that literally. He could have lived by keeping quiet. But he had things to say in his last year that he considered vital, things that it is dangerous to say, things that he knew it was dangerous to say—and still he put his life on the line for the right and opportunity to say them. To discard what Malcolm himself considered the most important part of his legacy, and for which he gave his life—that is indeed a sad mistake.

Despite my differences with Reverend Cleage's evaluation of Malcolm, which I have tried to present objectively and without personal rancor, I think I agree with what may have been the main intention of his talk three weeks ago. If I understood it correctly, his main intention was to inspire black people to make the Malcolm tradition their own—to interpret it according to their lights and needs, cherish it, make it a weapon in their struggle for freedom. With that intention I am in full accord.

I think this is already being done, to a far greater degree than Reverend Cleage does. The same night he spoke here, Eldridge Cleaver spoke in San Francisco about how the ideas and tradition of Malcolm have been "internalized" by black people all over the country. That is true, and in addition there is a growing body of written literature about Malcolm by black people, interpreting him and shaping his tradition, which Reverend Cleage overlooks or may not be aware of. On the West Coast there are people like Cleaver, not only writing about Malcolm but trying to continue what he began. In the Midwest, Milton Henry, Robert Higgins, Lerone Bennett, David Llorens. In the East, LeRoi Jones, Calvin Hernton, Rolland Snellings, Lawrence Neal, A.B. Spellman, Robert Allen, John 0. Killens, Robert Vernon, Sara Mitchell, C.E. Wilson—these are only a few of the many black people whose articles spring to mind (I hope the others will forgive me for not mentioning them too)— whose interpretations I may not always agree with, just as Reverend Cleage may not, but which show that black people have been doing what he urges, in sufficient quantity to fill many volumes. James

Baldwin is reportedly considering writing a play about Malcolm's *Autobiography;* a play called *Message from the Grass Roots* is soon to open in England. And the poets—I detected a slight tone of condescension or irony in Reverend Cleage's voice about the poetry by black people about Malcolm, a little surprising when you consider that in his profession he quotes poetry every Sunday—the poets too, in their own way, and it is not a way without influence, are making contributions to the preservation of the real Malcolm.

I agree, as I say, with what I take to be Reverend Cleage's intention. Malcolm is more than a hero and martyr, he is what Eldridge Cleaver calls "the standard" and "the model." I think he is and should be the standard and model for revolutionary and radical-minded people of all races, and will be for all who take the trouble to investigate him without prejudice and to learn from him. But he does belong, in a special sense, to black people first of all, and especially to young black people, whom Malcolm counted on to lead their people to freedom. If anyone should be the custodian of the Malcolm tradition it should be they.

Reverend Cleage called me the custodian, perhaps softening it a bit by granting my sincerity. To make sure, I looked up the world "custody" in the dictionary. It says: "1. keeping, guardianship, care: (example) *in the custody of her father;* 2. the keeping or charge of officers of the law: (example) *the car was in the custody of the police;* 3. imprisonment: (example) *he was taken into custody."* Well, I am not the custodian of the Malcolm tradition, I have not been, and I do not aspire to be. What I have been, or rather, what Marxists have been—because Reverend Cleage really means the Marxists rather than me personally—is (1) the chief *circulators* of the Malcolm material, and (2) *interpreters* of it, from our own point of view.

Circulators, because nobody else showed any interest in doing that job. Of this we are quite proud; we feel it has been a genuine contribution—but it is a task that we do and will gladly share with anyone else. The circulation of this material has been a contribution to everyone, black and white. It is the raw material—not distorted in any way, not dragged in, not partially presented or partially withheld to suit anybody's factional purposes—it is the raw material which everyone, white or black, can use in order to understand and then fashion the Malcolm tradition. In addition, as I said, we Marxists have interpreted the raw material—again, not by distorting what Malcolm said, only by giving our analysis and opinion about what he said and did. That is everybody's privilege, that is the duty of anybody who considers himself a radical, and we hope that all tendencies will work out and present their interpretations, as we have done, so that all interpretations can confront each other openly and provide a sound basis for what will be the historical judgment and tradition.

So I join with Reverend Cleage in urging black people to find out what Malcolm really said and stood for, write about it, preserve it, interpret it, circulate it, and use it in the struggle. All I say is that when you do this, don't do it partly—do it all the way; don't chop the Malcolm tradition to pieces—preserve the whole thing, confront the whole Malcolm, preserve the whole Malcolm, utilize the whole Malcolm to advance and win the struggle. If you do, and if your aim is to revolutionize society, then I think you will cherish the final part of the whole Malcolm, the part that he gave his life to add, as the most useful part because it is the most revolutionary.

5

More than one way
'to kill a Black man'

by George Breitman

This is a review of the book To Kill a Black Man by Louis E. Lomax (Holloway House, 1968). The first part was printed in the Militant, December 13, 1968; the second part appeared in the Young Socialist, February 1969.

THE SLANDERS OF A 'FRIEND'

The year 1968 has been a bad one for books about Malcolm X. First there was Archie Epps's *The Speeches of Malcolm X at Harvard*, mediocre as scholarship and absurd as analysis (see the *Militant*, August 9). Now there is Louis Lomax's book, which is even worse.

To Kill a Black Man is about Malcolm and Martin Luther King, both of whom Lomax knew. He began to write it shortly after Dr. King's assassination last April. This review will deal only with the parts about Malcolm, which take up about two-thirds of the book.

Most of what is good in this book is not new: Lomax borrows liberally from *The Autobiography of Malcolm X, Malcolm X Speaks, The Last Year of Malcolm X,* and his own 1963 work, *When the Word Is Given. . . .* And most of what is new in it is not good: the book contains many factual errors, contradictions, inconsistencies, exaggerations, and unverified or unverifiable assertions.

Some of the factual errors are involuntary; for example, Lomax says that Marcus Garvey "died in a con man's cell." As the term "con man" indicates, Lomax has a strong bias against Garvey. Perhaps that is why he relies on a poor memory of the black nationalist victim of U.S. government persecution, instead of looking up the fact that Garvey was released from prison in 1927 and did not die until 1940.

Other minor errors seem more calculated. Introducing the speech Malcolm gave in Detroit a week before his death, Lomax says, "I have elected to print it in its entirety." But in *Malcolm X Speaks*, from which Lomax took the Detroit speech, without credit to its source, there were eighteen different places in this speech where omissions were indicated (because those passages repeated points made in previous speeches in the book). Lomax has deleted those eighteen omission marks, showing he knew very well that he was not printing the entire speech.

Lomax's account of Malcolm's assassination is an example of his extreme irresponsibility. On one hand he says he is convinced that "the American government, particularly the CIA, was deeply involved in Malcolm's death," and on the other he accepts without question their version of who the hired killers were. "The men selected as Malcolm's assassins were ideal for the bloody task. They were affiliated with Elijah. . . ."[*]

He then tries to implicate "men very close to Malcolm" in the death plot, using nothing but the government's version as the basis for his accusation: ". . . three men well known to Malcolm and his

---

[*] The nearest thing to a public statement by the U.S. government was made by Carl Rowan, director of the U.S. Information Agency, speaking to the American Foreign Policy Association on February 25, 1965: "Mind you, here was a Negro who preached segregation and race hatred, killed by another Negro presumably from another organization that preaches segregation and race hatred, and neither of them representative of more than a tiny minority of the Negro population of America."—Ed.

aides—men who were then under indictment for the attempted murder of a Black Muslim defector—were allowed to enter the hall and obtain front row center seats and then carry out their mission of death. The very appearance of these men at the ballroom would have caused utmost security measures to go into effect had Malcolm's people been on the alert—or loyal!"

Lomax says he was Malcolm's friend, but there is nothing friendly, and much that is slanderous, in his treatment of Malcolm's alleged personal weaknesses. In the last period of his life, Lomax says, Malcolm was "confused," his "thoughts were in disarray," he was "obsessed" and "compulsively driven," and, to cap it all, "those who loved him felt he had cracked under the strain, that he was mentally ill."

Lomax charges Malcolm with "public duplicity" because he preached Black Muslim "dogmas many of us knew that he privately did not believe," and he promises to prove Malcolm "persisted in this behavior until the day of his death."

But all he shows is that, as a Black Muslim minister, Malcolm abided by the discipline and defended the ideas of his organization, even after he began to have doubts about some of them, because that was the only way he could remain in the Nation of Islam and work to reform it into an organization capable of leading the black liberation struggle. After he left the Black Muslims and was able to speak for himself, he had no reason to say things he was doubtful about or did not believe. Thereafter the things he said, whether right or wrong—and even though he may have changed his mind about them later—were the things he believed, and nothing else.

Lomax disputes Malcolm's statement that he became acquainted with Elijah Muhammad's teachings while he was in prison. He claims that long before, when Malcolm was a child, his half-sister, Ella Collins, was very close to Muhammad and "was scheduled to become Muhammad's first female minister"; and that it is "certain" Malcolm's father (who died when Malcolm was six) traveled to Detroit to "ponder the Black Muslim ideas." But what is "certain" in one sentence becomes merely an "assumption" in the next. Lomax claims to have obtained "new evidence" about these matters in January 1968, but he doesn't disclose the source of this so-called evidence, and the reader has no way of judging its validity.

Lomax uses this anonymous and therefore uncheckable "new evidence" device throughout the book, sometimes with ludicrous results. Thus, discussing the important turn Malcolm's thinking underwent after he left the Black Muslims, he says it is a question that has "haunted students of Malcolm for four years." Now they need be haunted no more because, he says, "I have encountered a few people who are now willing to disclose more information than that which came to the fore immediately after the assassination. I believe I now know what happened to Malcolm X; I think I can detail the corner he was attempting to turn."

His big revelation is that Malcolm began to move in the direction of socialism—something that has been well known since *Malcolm X Speaks* was published in 1965. *Everything* Lomax has to say on this is taken from the previously published literature. The "few people" he has encountered and "those who were closely allied" with Malcolm do not add a single scrap of information to what Malcolm himself said publicly in 1964–65.

But Lomax then uses the "authority" of these "sources" to peddle unadulterated fiction. An example is his treatment of the alliances Malcolm sought and made during his two trips to Africa in 1964, about which he did not speak in public, and which he may not have discussed in detail with any American after he came home.

According to Lomax, Malcolm went for help to the "Ben Bella-Nkrumah axis." He couldn't convince Ben Bella and Nkrumah "that the American black man was ready for revolution," but they agreed to supply him with funds after he showed results in America. An unnamed "source" told Lomax that Malcolm developed "deep doubts" about these "backers" in his last weeks and "was on the verge of reneging on certain commitments he made in Africa."

What were the commitments Malcolm allegedly made and allegedly was about to renege on? Only one is given: that Ben Bella and Nkrumah "exacted" from Malcolm a commitment to "rally the American black man and bring pressure against the American government to end its CIA activities in both Algeria and Ghana."

There are many ridiculous things in the book, but this is probably the worst, and surely the biggest insult to the intelligence of the reader with any political knowledge at all. Because Malcolm was an intransigent opponent of CIA and State Department counterrevolutionary activity not only in Algeria and Ghana, but everywhere in the world, and had been long before he ever saw Africa. A commitment to fight the CIA and State Department did not have to be "exacted" from him any more than he had to be pressured to breathe in and out. He could no more think of "reneging" on his long and open opposition to the agencies of U.S. imperialism than he could think of renouncing his struggle for Afro-American freedom.

It isn't necessary to go into reasons for doubting that Lomax is correct even about the identity of the people Malcolm sought as allies. The whole thing is such a cock-and-bull story that there is no reason to believe any part of it—just as there is no reason to believe any of the other gossip and guesses, throughout the book, that Lomax tries to palm off as "facts" and "new information."

IN DEFENSE OF MALCOLM X

Louis Lomax's book about Malcolm X (and Martin Luther King) is worthless as biography, history, or anything else. The trustworthy information in it is taken from other books. Lomax's own contributions consist of hunches and rumors paraded as "new information," which proves on examination to be as irresponsible as it is unreliable. Nevertheless, Lomax does discuss some questions worthy of attention, especially because many young people today do not know or remember what the situation was in Malcolm's last year; they were too young or had not yet become politically conscious.

For example: Malcolm X today is the hero of all young black militants and radicals. But things were different in the last year of his life (1964–65), when he had left the Nation of Islam and was trying to build a new movement. He had the respect of many black youth at that time, but not their organizational support or collaboration. Why?

Lomax lays the blame on Malcolm: he "failed to capture the confidence of his would-be followers"; he remained trapped in "myths" about black unity and internationalizing the struggle ("Malcolm would have done well to study the young students who were then plotting and planning. These black militants never wasted their time and mental powers discussing black unity"); he "was still talking loud without doing anything"; he lacked a program of action and was "philosophically confused," etc. As a result, "Malcolm had little, if any, rapport with the young black students who were then laying the foundations of the black power movement."

The above is about the first part of 1964, after Malcolm had left the Black Muslims. Referring to John Lewis and Donald Harris, who represented the Student Nonviolent Coordinating Committee on an African tour toward the end of 1964, Lomax says: ". . . after these ambassadors returned home they caucused with their fellow black militants. It is now clear that the decision was made to disrupt American cities. . . . Malcolm was never able to effect an alliance with the young black militants who were then plotting the crisis that is now upon the republic."

Let us leave aside the incredible accusation that the racial crisis is the result of a "plot" by SNCC or anyone else. Let us continue instead with Lomax's effort to explain why Malcolm did not win the young black militants to his movement.

A few months later, in February 1965, three days before his assassination, Malcolm appeared on a phone-in radio show, where the moderator tried to put some words about "revolution" in Malcolm's mouth. Malcolm refused to let him do it, and insisted on making the point he wanted to make. Lomax leaps upon this exchange as "abundantly clear" evidence of "why militant black youths refused to ally with Malcolm." Malcolm, he complains, "was clearly talking revolution but he would not advocate it. He refused to 'tell it like it is,' the only thing the young black militants welcome."[*]

What Lomax has constructed here is the story that Malcolm failed to win the young militants in 1964–65 because he was not as radical or revolutionary as they were. This story is absolutely false; like so much of the rest of the book, it has things upside down. The truth is just the opposite of what Lomax asserts—Malcolm had not won them (yet) because he was to their left at that time.

The first thing to be recalled is that the black power tendency did not arise until the middle of 1966, more than a year after Malcolm's death. It was initiated by leaders of SNCC and CORE, but these organizations had undergone considerable change, in both composition and outlook, since Malcolm's time.

Malcolm was an advocate of self-defense, while SNCC and CORE were then still under the influence of "nonviolence." Malcolm had been an opponent of the war in Vietnam from the beginning, but it was not until 1966 that SNCC and CORE came out against the war. Malcolm had opposed both capitalist parties in 1964, but SNCC and CORE were both working inside the Democratic Party that year; it was not until after Malcolm's death that Stokely Carmichael went to Alabama to help the black people of Lowndes County break with the Democratic Party and build a party of their own.

Carmichael, in fact, is a good example to clarify the real relationship. This is not recalled in order to belittle him in any way, but it is a fact that in Malcolm's last year Carmichael was still hostile to him, as is documented in the interview Carmichael gave Robert Penn Warren (*Who Speaks for the Negro?*, 1965). In this he was only reflecting the attitudes of the other young leaders of SNCC and CORE at that time, about whom Malcolm spoke with respect, but who had not yet made their break with liberalism.

After Malcolm died, that generation of black youth did move rapidly to the left, many of them to a revolutionary position. Mal-

---

[*] Relevant excerpts from this radio show, which took place February 18, 1965, will be found under the title "Confrontation with an 'Expert'" in *Malcolm X Speaks*.—Ed.

colm had been expecting this, and counting on it to build his movement, but it did not occur until after his death.

If Lomax's memory of the black youth in Malcolm's last year is
worthless, his assessment of Malcolm as a revolutionary is even worse.

When Malcolm left the Black Muslims in March 1964, he began
to move to the left, and, especially after his trips to Africa that year,
began to develop and present revolutionary, internationalist, anticapitalist, and prosocialist positions. All this is documented in
Malcolm X Speaks and *The Last Year of Malcolm X.*

Lomax accepts the material in those books, and even repeats some
of their terminology. But he isn't content to do just that—this know-
it-all opponent of revolution also has to deliver some lectures about
what Malcolm should have done to become a better and more successful revolutionary.

So, discussing the period shortly after the Black Muslim split,
when Malcolm was beginning his search for a program and cadres
to build a new kind of movement, Lomax says: "Malcolm was still
talking loud without doing anything. He failed to listen to his own
dissertation on the nature of a true revolution; a people cannot
carry out a revolution by rhetoric! Had Malcolm, instead, marshaled
what forces he had at his command, selected a clear-cut goal and
announced that if the evil was not corrected within, say, ten days,
all hell would break loose in New York City—well, had Malcolm
done that he would have changed the course of his own life and the
pace of American history as well."

That's what a Lomax would have done, if somehow he wanted to
play the role of a "revolutionary." A people cannot carry out a revolution by rhetoric—but they can carry it out by bluff! Lomax does
not tell us what Malcolm should have done after the bluff was called.

But Malcolm was not a bluffer, and he very much wanted to avoid
being considered one. At the time Lomax is talking about, Malcolm
had only a few dozen people in the Muslim Mosque, Incorporated
(he had not yet formed the nonreligious Organization of Afro-
American Unity); many people in Harlem were sympathetic, but
would not join yet, and could not be counted on. Nothing would

Speaking to young militants in Selma, Alabama, February 4, 1965, during voter registration struggle.

have been more disastrous to this fledgling movement than the kind of adventurist tactics recommended by Lomax.

The task Malcolm faced at that time was to consolidate a movement, to educate, train, and develop a nucleus of leaders, to knit them together with *ideas*—not with suicidal adventures. A people cannot carry out a revolution by rhetoric, but a leader can start a revolutionary movement by speaking, by propaganda—provided the propaganda is revolutionary and capable of attracting the forces that later can make the revolution.

That's what Malcolm was trying to do in that period. If he had followed the advice Lomax now offers, he certainly would have changed the course of his life—by making a laughingstock of himself. Fortunately, Malcolm was more realistic about the needs and possibilities of the difficult situation he was in after the split.

Malcolm believed in "some action," but he wanted what he called "intelligent action"—that is, mass action—well thought out in advance, prepared, and launched under the most favorable circumstances. He did not believe in leading people into a bloodbath for the sake of the excitement or of something to do. He always defended the oppressed in any clash with the oppressors, but that doesn't mean he advocated clashes where the oppressed would suffer the most casualties. He was in Africa in July 1964, when the police launched their reign of terror in the so-called Harlem riot. Malcolm defended resistance to the police in that "pogrom," as he called it; but he also revealed, after his return home, that he had known in advance that the police were planning such an assault, and that he had advised his co-workers against recklessly giving the police any pretexts to destroy the movement.

A revolutionary chooses his own time and place, insofar as he can. He seizes hold of some opportunities, he avoids others. He does not simply raise his voice and give a command when the probable result will be broken heads for the people he wants to educate and organize to take on the strongest government in the world. That's the difference, or one difference, between a genuine revolutionary and a middle-class liberal indulging in fantasies about revolution.

As previously mentioned, three days before his death Malcolm refused to let the moderator of a radio show put words in his mouth about revolution. We have already quoted Lomax's remark that "Malcolm was clearly talking revolution but he would not advocate it." Then he continues: "Only Allah knows what Malcolm's final fears were; perhaps the possibility of being charged with sedition deterred him. Whatever the reason Malcolm forewent an excellent opportunity to flatly state that what is needed in this country is a revolution. Had Malcolm said it, and had luck been with him, the federal government would have arrested him. Alas, that sequence of events would have catapulted him into the black leadership position for which he had hungered for so long. But Malcolm continued to seek some kind of accommodation with the power structure. He was all too deliberate in his efforts to obey the law and order, a gesture no revolutionary can afford."

Since Malcolm was clearly "talking revolution," as Lomax admits, then why this big stress on his not advocating it at that particular moment? Malcolm advocated revolution plenty of times during his last year—flatly, squarely, roundly, and every other way. (By Lomax's logic, he had no "luck" on those occasions because he wasn't arrested.) And even when he didn't advocate it formally, everybody in his audiences knew what he was talking about.

Only an ass would propose that Malcolm should have invited, or been indifferent to, government prosecution; or would contend that getting arrested was the easy road to a "leadership position"; or would charge that Malcolm's carefully thought-out ("deliberate") choice of words and formulations, designed to make it harder for the government to attack his movement legally, represented some kind of "accommodation with the power structure."

As a matter of fact, young revolutionists today can benefit from a study of the way Malcolm got the most radical ideas across to his audiences. He was a master of the use of defensive formulations, which never conceded an inch in principle to the government and yet never gave the government any weapons or pretexts for legal action against his movement. To survive, genuine revolutionaries must learn flexible tactics as well as irreconcilable principles—even though that may deprive them of the Lomaxian seal of approval.

Lomax's statement that Malcolm "continued" to seek accommodation with the power structure (by not issuing ultimatums or using the language Lomax thinks he should have used) is part of his pattern of casting doubt of Malcolm's revolutionary integrity and consistency. There are other passages of the same type: "The final Malcolm was a man whose revolutionary rhetoric was tempered by the ethics of the corrupt society he sought to depose. On Saturday morning (the day before his death) Malcolm moved even deeper into the framework of the "American ethic" by deciding "to buy a house in an integrated, predominantly Jewish, section of Long Island, New York."

Malcolm's home had been bombed early that week, his family escaping death or injury by pure luck; and the courts had ordered his eviction from the home originally provided by the Black Muslims. Nobody would rent to him after the bombing, he needed a home in a hurry, and he found one in a neighborhood where he thought it would be harder for a new bombing to be attempted. It was a decision to provide a roof and perhaps greater safety for his children. To cite this practical, tactical, decision as a sign that Malcolm was capitulating to "the American ethic" is so vile that it's hard to find the right word for it.

And at the end of the book Lomax says, "The irony of Malcolm was that he embraced the notion of love at a time in history when it became fashionable for black men to openly express their hate. . . . And at a time when his only hope of realizing full power lay in issuing the bold call for out and out revolution Malcolm began to articulate the ethic of brotherhood."

But a week before his death, Malcolm said in Detroit (and Lomax reprinted it): "I'm for brotherhood for everybody, but I don't believe in forcing brotherhood upon people who don't want it. Let us practice brotherhood among ourselves, and then if others want to practice brotherhood with us, we're for practicing it with them also. But I don't think that we should run around trying to love somebody who doesn't love us."

There is no inconsistency whatever between that conception of brotherhood and the view Malcolm held to his last hour: that a social revolution against capitalism is needed to abolish racism. Lomax's attempt to confuse his readers on this point is part of his overall aim—to destroy the stature of a black revolutionary. There is more than one way "to kill a black man."

6

A liberal supports
the government version

by George Breitman

This three-part review of The Death and Life of Malcolm X by Peter Goldman (Harper & Row, 1973) was first published in the Militant, February 23, March 2, and March 9, 1973.

REVOLUTIONARY OR PROPHET?

Peter Goldman, a reporter when he first interviewed Malcolm X in 1962 and now a senior editor at *Newsweek,* insists on calling this "a white book about Malcolm X . . . written from a white perspective." He would have done better to call it a white liberal book, from a white liberal perspective; and since Black and white liberals share basic assumptions, it would have been even more accurate to say a liberal book and a liberal perspective.

Liberals have changed many of their ideas since 1962, especially about race relations; they used to think everything would be taken care of by passing a few laws, and now many of them think nothing can be done, and have stopped trying. Goldman has not become quite that pessimistic, but in most other respects he remains a typical liberal. He was strongly influenced by Malcolm, and he tries to pay tribute to his memory by telling the truth about him. But the truth as he sees it is blurred, and in some places stood on its head, by his incorrigible liberal biases.

A clear example of this is the way he presents Malcolm's views on independent Black political action in 1964 after Malcolm had left the Nation of Islam—views that remained unchanged until Malcolm's death the following year: "He was adamantly against registering black people as Democrats or Republicans, a commitment that struck him as a sellout in advance. There was a vein of political naiveté in this, since most of the real political decisions in Harlem are taken by signed-up Democrats in Democratic clubhouses and Democratic primaries; to register blacks as independents would, whatever its spiritual satisfaction, cut them out of the real electoral process."

For most liberals political action means being part of the Democratic Party. They simply cannot understand how anyone fails to see this. In their minds people who think of political action in any other terms are blind, retarded, or naive. Malcolm was breaking with this conception and trying to move the Black masses in another direction. His reasons for doing so were *political*. But Goldman, when he tries to explain Malcolm's position, is capable only of suggesting that it may have given him "spiritual satisfaction" to attack the two-party system that oppresses Blacks.

Not all of Goldman's liberal prejudices are as glaring as that one. Some are not of much importance, but others have a ruinous effect on his attempts to understand and explain what Malcolm was trying to do, especially in his last year.

In part, Goldman's book is a polemic against the conclusions reached in my book, *The Last Year of Malcolm X,* which was completed in the spring of 1966. He calls it "an ingeniously done Marxist analysis, purporting to show that Malcolm was evolving into a prosocialist, anticapitalist revolutionary. . . . My own feeling is that the book is too narrow and schematic a treatment of Malcolm's lively and free-running intelligence. . . ."

Leaving aside questions of tone, style, or method, let's try to stick with the substantive questions—was Malcolm a revolutionary in his last year or not? Here's how Goldman handles that: "He thought of himself as a teacher, a minister, a Muslim, an African, an internationalist, and in the most general terms a revolutionary; and, before any of these things, as black." But the fact that he thought of himself as (and was) many things did not make him any the less a revolutionary.

"He talked about revolution, without defining either its means (except that it probably wouldn't be nonviolent) or its ends (beyond 'respect and recognition' for black people)." I think that most objective readers of *Malcolm X Speaks* or *By Any Means Necessary* would consider that a bad distortion.

"His radicalism directed itself only gradually or fragmentarily at the basic institutions of American democracy and American capitalism; Malcolm attacked those institutions savagely for their hypocrisies and cruelties, but he accepted them then [March 1964] as given and proposed that they might even be used." Why the "but"? Every intelligent revolutionary accepts the institutions of capitalism as "given," until they are replaced, and everyone but infantile ultraleftists tries to make use of some (elections, legal action, etc.) whenever that will benefit the revolutionary cause.

"He was a revolutionary without an army, or an ideology, or any clear sense of how the revolution was to be waged and what it would do if it won. Malcolm, instead, was a revolutionary of the spirit, which is the most subversive sort of all; he was interested less in overthrowing institutions than in undermining the assumptions on which our institutions have run." A revolutionary of the spirit (only), that is, one who has no clear sense of revolutionary principles, strategy, or tactics, is usually acceptable to the liberals. It makes you wonder why the liberals almost without exception wouldn't have *anything* to do with Malcolm in his last year.

Although he doesn't say so flatly and cleanly, Goldman is admitting in the passages cited that Malcolm was some sort of revolutionary. So let's see next what he does about the adjectives prosocialist and anticapitalist.

Writing about Malcolm on his return from Mecca and Africa in the spring of 1964, Goldman says: "He did come home impressed by his glimpse of socialism and his introduction to its vocabulary. He worked some of it tentatively into a few speeches and interviews, arguing that racism wasn't the only problem—that it was the handmaiden of colonialism and capitalism." The key words for Goldman there are "tentatively" and "few." "One guesses that Malcolm's interest in African socialism at that point was more that it was African than that it was socialist; it was in any case a minor motif in his speeches." There it's "minor."

Goldman then uncritically cites some condescending testimony from Charles Silberman about a radio panel on which he and Malcolm spoke in June 1964: "I got the feeling that he [Malcolm] really didn't know what he meant by the [radical] words [he used] and that he didn't have any real conviction about them. He was trying out any idea that would come to him and asking himself, 'Is this the way I go?' I remember thinking he was really floundering."

"Or improvising," Goldman adds. "Socialism remained a downtown idea and a downtown theme for Malcolm. . . ." (Downtown here means not in Harlem.)

But, Goldman has to add in a later chapter, "A strand of Left rhetoric did appear in some of Malcolm's later speeches and interviews, particularly but not exclusively downtown. He continued to see color as central but not necessarily the single motive force in his world: Malcolm began arguing that the nonwhite people of the world had not only their nonwhiteness in common but their exploitation by the West. Occasionally, he identified capitalism straight out as an enemy—'You show me a capitalist, I'll show you a bloodsucker'—and socialism as the almost universal system among the new Third World nations coming into independence." Quite a strand.

Goldman doesn't take this seriously, however; whatever clashes with his prejudices can easily be labeled "rhetoric." Furthermore, he assures us, "his Left language and Left themes were hardly more than asides for Malcolm—and in his very last speeches and interviews they abruptly vanished." He then proceeds to speculate about why Malcolm's radical "rhetoric" vanished from his last speeches.

Malcolm with Clifton DeBerry, Socialist Workers Party's 1964 candidate for President.

We need not bother with his speculations here because the statement itself is simply untrue. Malcolm's last complete speech, three days before his death, was at Columbia University, where he said, "We are living in an age of revolution, and the revolt of the American Negro is part of the rebellion against the oppression and colonialism which has characterized this era. . . . It is incorrect to classify the revolt of the Negro as simply a racial conflict of black against white, or as a purely American problem. Rather, we are today seeing a global rebellion of the oppressed against the oppressor, the exploited against the exploiter."

For some reason (his own politics?), Goldman seems driven to belittle any and every sign that Malcolm was becoming prosocialist. For him, they are at most "bits of socialism in his late vocabulary, whatever they may have signaled about his thinking." He even offers a kind of "logic" for his stubbornness on this point: "Having once indentured his soul to a particular leader [Muhammad] and a particular dogma [that of the Nation of Islam], he would not have done so again [indenture his soul to socialism or other "dogmas"]." This aspect of Goldman's Malcolm ends up somehow more like Goldman than Malcolm.

Goldman does not seem aware of what he is doing, perhaps, but in his eagerness to minimize Malcolm's interest in socialism and revolutionary ideas generally, he succeeds in disparaging Malcolm's intelligence and integrity: "Malcolm had only a provisional public philosophy in those days [March 1964]—not so much a single, coherent system of thought as a loosely strung set of positions that were changing even as he announced them. . . ."

"The truth, as Malcolm himself kept telling us, was that he didn't know where he was going or what he wanted to be, except *flexible*."

"His ideology and his program, to the extent that he had any. . . . [May 1964]"

"That new politics [which Malcolm was trying to create in his last months] remained a composite rather than a system—a loosely strung series of positions held together more by Malcolm's militant bearing than by any single coherent philosophy."

"He was not a saint, really; neither was he a strategist or a semi-nal thinker or even a major leader. . . . Malcolm X was something more important than any of these things. He was a prophet."

"He made substantial contributions to what is now orthodox Black Thought—the stresses on land, power, community control, national identity, Pan-Africanism, the right to self-defense. . . . But his more important legacy was his example, his bearing, his affir-mation of blackness. . . ."

Goldman thinks Malcolm was a great man, but not because of his ideas during his last year. Malcolm, by contrast, thought those ideas important enough to risk his life for.

Fortunately, the major speeches and statements of Malcolm's last year are in print, and the reader can consult them to make indepen-dent judgments about the issues discussed above. Unfortunately, there are two other issues discussed in Goldman's book that cannot be tested in this way—the internal life and problems of the organi-zations Malcolm created after he left the Black Muslims, and the assassination of Malcolm. I say unfortunately because in my opin-ion Goldman is not only wrong in the way he handles them, but irresponsible as well.

THE OAAU AND THE MMI

When Malcolm X left the Nation of Islam in March 1964, he formed an organization called the Muslim Mosque, Incorporated, through which he hoped to build a new kind of movement for Black libera-tion. But he soon realized that the religious nature and name of the MMI was a handicap to recruiting the non-Muslim and non-reli-gious masses he wanted to enlist. So he founded another group in June 1964—the nonsectarian Organization of Afro-American Unity, which served as the principal arena for his organizational activities until his assassination in February 1965. This led to a certain amount of dissension among his supporters, some of whom thought a reli-gious cover provided protection against government harassment and repression.

I knew in 1966, when I wrote *The Last Year of Malcolm X*, that prior to Malcolm's death both of his organizations had been gripped by factional strife. One group held that Malcolm and his supporters should have restricted their activities to a "religious base" and abstained from "politics." The other group held a contrary view— that more and better politics was needed; it included both those who were orienting toward what they considered to be revolutionary politics and those whose ideas about politics were rudimentary.

In the introduction to my book I made brief mention of these differences among Malcolm's collaborators. I did not feel I could go beyond that because the people involved were unwilling at that time to discuss the differences with nonmembers. Since then I have learned more about the internal life and problems of the OAAU and MMI, a subject I consider very important, but still not enough to make me feel qualified to write on it.

One reason why I looked forward to the new book by Peter Goldman was the advance report that it was based on almost a hundred interviews that he had held, with Malcolm's associates among others, during his three years of work on the book. I hoped that at last long-needed light was going to be cast on a vital aspect of Malcolm's last year.

But Goldman doesn't do this—partly because he just isn't interested in the problems of building the kind of movement Malcolm was trying to build (how could he be if he thinks that the important thing about Malcolm was that he was a "prophet"?) and partly because he takes it for granted that the "religion" faction was right and the "politics" faction was wrong.

At any rate, only one side of the dispute gets a hearing in this book. Among Malcolm's lieutenants who are quoted by name, the chief are Benjamin Goodman and Charles 37X Kenyatta, both of whom, although not for the same reasons, were bitterly and increasingly dissatisfied with Malcolm's course beginning with the foundation of the OAAU. (Sometimes I tend to think that there wasn't a "politics" faction with a clear orientation of its own so much as a group that supported Malcolm's political approach against its critics inside the two organizations.)

Goldman doesn't mention it, but Benjamin Goodman has decided since Malcolm's death that the whole split with the Nation of Islam was a mistake and has made conciliatory gestures toward Elijah Muhammad (see his introduction to *The End of White World Supremacy,* his 1971 collection of Malcolm's speeches as a Black Muslim). Goldman does mention that Kenyatta appeared as a witness for the defense at the 1966 Malcolm murder trial, where he sought to bolster the defense "theory" that members of the "politics" faction had murdered Malcolm; but he doesn't mention that Kenyatta's own politics subsequently led him to support the election of New York Governor Nelson Rockefeller.

It was perfectly proper for Goldman to learn everything he could from people like Goodman and Kenyatta and to quote their opinions and arguments. But why was he so uncritical about what they told him? And why are all the other (unnamed) OAAU members whom he quotes supporters of the "religion" faction? To the latter question, he may reply that they were the only ones who would talk to him. In that case, he should have said so, explicitly alerting the reader to the fact that he is presenting only one side of the dispute—the side, incidentally, which he happens to sympathize with.

Goldman's failure to do that will mislead many readers. It has even disoriented Goldman. "The OAAU was the worst mistake we ever made," he quotes one of the "religion" group as telling him. "At the very end," Goldman adds, "Malcolm himself came to agree and ordered its thorough overhaul." This is a monstrous misstatement of fact. Malcolm was critical about the OAAU's weaknesses and was actively trying to get them corrected, but he *never* thought and *never* said that creating it was the worst mistake they had ever made. Goldman knows quite well that it is journalistically irresponsible to attribute such a belief to Malcolm on the basis of the flimsy, one-sided hearsay evidence that is all he has in this case.

Almost as bad—not quite, but almost—is the way he escalates gossip into seeming fact. First we are told that Malcolm's friends (that is, people who were dragging their feet or actively obstructing his course inside their movement) "suggest" that in his last days he gave up his radical "rhetoric" because "he had begun to feel crowded by his new vocabulary and his new comrades and that he was trying at the end to disengage from them." We've already shown that there is no truth in the story about the "abrupt vanishing" of Malcolm's radicalism, but that's not the point here.

Goldman is very quick to respond to the "suggestion" of the "friends." On his own, he now asserts, "At the very end, he seemed to be moving away from Marx to Allah—to the mosque as his real base of operations." He sees different ways of explaining this—for example, "one can read it as a withdrawal from a system of thought and a society of men that had grown claustrophobic for him—a strait jacket as constricting as the one he had just shucked off." But by now the suggestion has for Goldman acquired all the weight of virtual fact. The phrase "away from Marx to Allah" is so irresistible to him that he forgets he has been denying all along that Malcolm was ever anywhere near Marx.

Malcolm's real attitude to his so-called new vocabulary and so-called new friends (code names for socialism and revolutionary socialists he was willing to collaborate with) can be discovered in two ways. One is by learning the truth about the situation inside the OAAU and the MMI. The other is by learning how and to what degree Malcolm and his socialist collaborators worked together. About the first I don't know enough, and I have learned very little from Goldman's book. About the second I know enough to say that the version presented by Goldman and the "friends" is utterly worthless.

Anyone who wants to get a sample picture of the relations between Malcolm and the SWP and the Young Socialist Alliance should read the 1966 article "Two Interviews" by Jack Barnes, reprinted as an appendix in *The Last Year of Malcolm X*. This account of the relations that existed less than a month before Malcolm's assassination makes it perfectly clear that those relations were based on mutual respect and mutual trust, were entirely voluntary on both sides, and depended first of all on Malcolm's initiative. All suggestions about Malcolm feeling crowded, claustrophobic, or constricted by these relations are the products of political malice, political ignorance, or both.

A 'SCENARIO' OF THE ASSASSINATION

A large part of Peter Goldman's book is devoted to the assassination of Malcolm X in February 1965, the ensuing police investigation, and the trial where three men were convicted of the crime in 1966. Here these subjects get the most extensive treatment they have had in any book to date.

Unfortunately, Goldman is hobbled by a thesis he is determined to prove: he did not believe when he began his inquiries, and he does not believe today, that the U.S. government had or could have had any hand in the assassination. He finds the government and its police not guilty, and he accepts their version that Malcolm was killed by three members of the Nation of Islam, at the instigation of unnamed officials of the Nation (although he admits that the prosecution's version of the events as presented in the court was somewhat "tidied up").

"My inquiry," he tells us, "was limited by my own resources, and no doubt also by my color, class, politics, and a certain irremediable skepticism about conspiratorialist explanations of events where non-conspiratorialist explanations appear to be adequate." The factors that reinforced his "skepticism" were undoubtedly his middle-class outlook and the liberal politics that flow so naturally from it.

Goldman simply can't believe that the government would do such a thing as participate in the murder of Malcolm. Granted that the government didn't like him, and granted that it gets dangerous people out of the way; it does this, however, he says, "not by some conspiratorial grand design and not ordinarily by murdering them" but through "the far more common sanctions" of "prison and/or exile."

This expression of faith in the nonmurderous character of the government is very touching, and explains a lot about Goldman. But it doesn't prove anything. The government usually resorts to frame-up and prison, but it isn't restricted to them. Not long before Malcolm's death the government approved the assassination of Ngo Dinh Diem, president of South Vietnam. Was Malcolm's life more sacred in the government's eyes than Diem's? All that need be said on this subject is that while assassination is not the government's normal method of repression, it *is* one of its methods. Excluding this possibility is not a promising way to begin an investigation of Malcolm's assassination.

While Goldman merely exonerates the federal government, he positively glows with admiration for the police and prosecutors who prepared the case for trial. Some of them gave him interviews for this book, and they emerge as salt of the earth. Oh, a little cynical perhaps, a little too inclined to cut corners, but otherwise splendid chaps: dedicated to the cause of justice ("Hardly anybody slept at all the first two or three nights, and after that you napped at the squad or Manhattan North when you could and got home long enough to shower and change clothes and just miss seeing the kids off to school"), hard-working (Detective Keeley "worked sixteen hours a day, seven days a week for seven straight weeks before he got his first day off"), generous to the point of self-sacrifice (Goldman thinks they pay with cash out of their own pockets for tips from informers, his evidence being one detective who told him, "I put out maybe a thousand dollars for stoolies [in the Malcolm investigation]. A case like that can put you in the poorhouse.").

All in all, Goldman says, "they conducted a conscientious investigation under extraordinarily difficult circumstances." But at most his book shows why the jury voted to convict the three men indicted by the government, and even that isn't done with complete adequacy.

The prosecution had many advantages at the trial—plentiful funds and personnel to work up and "tidy up" a case. Its legal power enabled it to threaten witnesses with arrest if they did not "cooperate." Goldman indicates the police may have threatened Malcolm's associates with arrest in connection with the fire bombing of Harlem Mosque No. 7 shortly after the assassination: "An arson charge can serve you better as a persuader—a legal blunt instrument that can get people talking and doesn't leave any marks." The police actually did imprison the chief prosecution witness for almost a year before the trial, dropping charges against him after he cooperated at the trial. They also benefited strongly from the then widespread prejudice against the Black Muslims.

But the chief advantage the prosecution had was the defense counsel's incompetence and unwillingness to fight. This was particularly true of the four lawyers for the two Black Muslim defendants, Norman 3X Butler and Thomas 15X Johnson. To show that they lacked "the cash for a wide-ranging investigation," Goldman mentions that these four were "court-appointed at the statutory fee of $2,000 per man." But he misses the main point of the fact he cites.

In New York, as in most big cities, court appointment jobs are viewed by all concerned as political plums, despite the relatively low fee. They are given to reliable people, that is, people who do not rock the boat. They don't get such plums from the dominant political machine by trying to prove in court, for example, that the government and police are in collusion in an assassination; if they do that once, they do it knowing they'll never get such an appointment again.

That was why these court-appointed lawyers had to cook up the theory, accepted by hardly anyone but the Black Muslims and Bayard Rustin, that Malcolm had been killed by disgruntled members of his own organization. That was why these lawyers did such a poor job in cross-examining the well-coached witnesses for the prosecution. That—and not the compelling logic of the prosecution's case—was basically why the jury voted to convict Butler, Johnson, and Talmadge Hayer. (Hayer had confessed his own part in the murder but wouldn't name his accomplices. He did say, however, that they were not Butler and Johnson.)

So Goldman's "skepticism" spares the defense counsel as well as the government and the police. It is reserved almost exclusively for the "true disbelievers," those who reject the government's version and suspect the government and the police were involved in the murder conspiracy. He lumps together all who will not accept the government version; in his opinion they are all irrational or dishonest.

But he singles out as the "principal conspiratorialist treatments" articles in the *Militant* by me in 1965, a few months after the assassination, by Herman Porter in 1966, during the trial (together published as a pamphlet entitled *The Assassination of Malcolm X**), and an article by Eric Norden in *The Realist,* February 1967. "Breitman-Porter is the soberer, Norden the more fanciful," Goldman writes; "both are wanting in objective reporting and both accordingly are stuck with the fictitious Second Suspect as the major single piece of 'evidence' of a state conspiracy."

But Goldman has labored in vain if he thinks his book will persuade rational and honest people to swallow the government version or give the government and police a clean bill of health. Before explaining why, I want to review the way he has answered or discussed some of the questions that we raised in 1965 and 1966.

On the night of the assassination, the three New York morning papers all reported that two suspects had been arrested at the Audubon Ballroom; Talmadge Hayer by two cops in a scout car that happened accidentally to be passing by, and an unnamed person by Patrolman Thomas Hoy, the only policeman stationed outside the Audubon at the time of the killing. The second editions of these same papers all changed their stories, stating only that Hayer had been captured and not even mentioning the second man. In fact, they never mentioned him again.

Thinking that to be an unusual journalistic procedure, I asked publicly for an explanation. To my knowledge none was ever given in print before Goldman's book. The prosecution's version at the trial, of course, was that only one man had been arrested at the Audubon—Hayer. But it did not call Patrolman Hoy as a witness (neither did the defense).

---

* Chapters 2 and 3 of this book—Ed.

Now Goldman tells us that it was all a journalistic mix-up—that the man Hoy caught was the same one that the other two cops took into custody.* He does not provide details, although his book has room for much trivia, and he does not explain why none of the newspapers bothered to make an explicit correction at the time. But even so, Goldman's version is not unreasonable: it could have happened the way he says. Granting that, however, is not the same as granting that the "second suspect" is "the major single piece of 'evidence' of a state conspiracy."

Twelve days before his assassination Malcolm flew to Paris to speak at a meeting, as he had done three months before without incident. This time he was barred from the country as "undesirable." The French government's explanation was that Malcolm's speech could have "provoked demonstrations that would trouble the public order." After the assassination Malcolm's friends in Paris charged that the French government really had barred him because it thought he would be assassinated on French soil and did not want to bear the onus for such a scandal.

Calling it an unverified rumor, I reported this charge in the *Militant* and asked the press to check it out. If the charge was true, I said, it was important to know why the French government expected a murder attempt, from whom it expected one, and where it got its information. One thing was certain—the Black Muslims did not have the resources to organize an assassination in France.

Goldman rejects the implications from that fact, which pointed to possible CIA complicity. "A more credible version," he writes, "was that the French acted on the representation of two of their

---

* In a footnote, Goldman explains away the second suspect on the basis of information supplied by the police: "Hoy and Aronoff [the arresting officers at the assassination scene] were debriefed separately at the time, Hoy at the scene and Aronoff at the stationhouse, and the early editions of the next day's papers reported that there had been two arrests. The two policemen, as it developed, were talking about the same man, but the confusion lasted long enough to create a whole folklore around the 'arrest' of a mysterious Second Suspect—a mythology that endures to this day."—Ed.

lately liberated colonies, Senegal and the Ivory Coast, that Malcolm—aided and abetted by Nasser and Nkrumah—might try to overthrow moderate, pro-Western governments like their own." Goldman can only deplore the French government's "lack of official candor" and the "tact that forbade anyone's saying so [about Senegal and the Ivory Coast] at the time" because these things have "nourished the conspiratorialist theory of Malcolm's assassination ever since. . . ."

This version is not only more credible (to Goldman) but later he elevates it a little and calls it "most probable." For evidence, he tells us that his account "is based on unpublished reporting in *Newsweek's* files." But we aren't told who did the reporting, where the reporters got their information, and why (besides "tact") the reporting was not published.

Gullible people may accept this kind of stuff, but others will say it's no more convincing than the kind of evidence Goldman rejects as flimsy when advanced by "conspiratorialists." On the face of it, Goldman's version is no more credible than the one put forward by Malcolm's friends in Paris. He has merely suggested another possibility. When I do that, and my possibility points toward the government, that's conspiratorialist; when he does it, and his possibility points away from the government, it's objective reporting, or something of that sort.

I wrote in 1965 that I did not know if Butler and Johnson had any connection with the assassination but strongly doubted they had themselves been present in the Audubon. They were Black Muslims well known to Malcolm's people and therefore could expect to be stopped at the door, questioned, and probably searched by the guards if they had tried to enter the meeting hall.

At the trial the prosecution produced witnesses who swore they saw Butler and Johnson present and shooting at Malcolm. But knowing how the prosecution obtained such testimony and reading of the many contradictions in that testimony leaves me still dubious. It is not impossible that they were present, but to believe it I would have to see or hear some evidence that *they* thought they would be admitted, and a theory explaining *why* they thought so.

This is one of several questions we raised before the trial that were not answered satisfactorily at the trial and that Goldman concedes are still unanswered or troubling today. But they don't trouble him enough to affect his final verdict. When he mentions them, it's proof of his open-mindedness and objectivity. When we mention them, it's proof of paranoia, distortion, etc.

To summarize: Goldman scores a few points, suggests new possibilities on some, and misses the mark altogether on others. That he fails in his main objective I shall now try to show by presenting a "scenario" of the assassination that is not in contradiction with any of the facts reported in his book.

Around a month before the assassination the police learned of a plot to kill Malcolm. (That's what they said.) How they learned they never said. It could be they learned about it because one or more agents of the conspiracy were members of the police. (It is known that they had infiltrated agents into the Nation of Islam, Malcolm's organizations, and other militant groups. One of these, Gene Roberts, became part of the top OAAU leadership, it was revealed in 1970 at the New York Black Panther trial.)

The Bureau of Special Services (BOSS), which was the name of the New York secret police agency at the time, must have communicated this information to Washington, that is, the CIA, because the CIA's keen interest in Malcolm was publicly known. We can assume that the CIA was consulted on and approved, if it did not suggest, the policy then pursued by the BOSS officials, which was to offer Malcolm police protection after having concluded he would have to reject it for political reasons. When Malcolm or a lieutenant did refuse, the man from BOSS told Goldman, "as far as I was concerned, that took us off the hook."

Talmadge Hayer, it is safe to assume, was a member of the murder gang. Whether some or all of the other members were Black Muslims, or ex-Black Muslims, we cannot say, but in this context that question is not decisive. The important thing was that at some point it was decided to proceed with the Malcolm killing. The BOSS agent or agents, assuming for the sake of argument that they were involved, might have taken the initiative in this decision; at the least they would have supported it and made themselves useful in obtaining weapons, devising tactics, raising morale, and encouraging the project in other ways. (This is precisely what the BOSS agent was doing then in the concurrent "Statue of Liberty conspiracy.")

The CIA/BOSS officials did not try to break up the murder gang. On the contrary, they told their agent(s) to proceed with business as usual, that is, to help the plot develop. The agent(s) provided the weapons and—more important—inside information (from BOSS agents in the OAAU) about the OAAU and its security methods, and an assassination plan in accord with that information that offered a good possibility that all of the killers could escape after the murder. (They all did, except Hayer, who might well have gotten away too if one of Malcolm's guards had not shot him in the leg.)

The CIA/BOSS officials did not have to organize a murder gang from scratch and in their own name—they found one ready-made. This was an advantage because the participants (except for the agent or agents) wouldn't even know whose interests they were serving. (In this case, the full story may not be disclosed even if Talmadge Hayer decides to talk.) The CIA/BOSS officials did not have to give the order, "Kill Malcolm." All they had to do was let their agents proceed as usual, and wait for the bloody outcome. They were "off the hook" after their offer of police protection was rejected. But that particular assassination might have been stopped if they had tried to stop it, and therefore they were just as guilty of the assassination as the men who pulled the triggers.

This "scenario" explains many things that are otherwise inexplicable: why the killers were so audacious, why seventeen of the twenty cops in the special detail assigned to the Audubon were so far from the scene of the crime, why the government felt no qualms about prosecuting Hayer once he was caught at the scene, why it did not produce any BOSS agents as witnesses at the trial, and why it did not produce the Malcolm guard charged with shooting Hayer. It may also help explain why the police publicly accused Malcolm of having fire bombed his own home when his family was asleep in it a week before the assassination. And it definitely disposes of many objections like the so-called "clincher": *Can you imagine the CIA hiring somebody like Hayer?*—because Hayer didn't have to be paid by the CIA to do what the CIA wanted done.

So the argument pointing to the CIA and the police is much more plausible than Goldman makes it out to be in his book, even if his explanation about the second suspect is accepted. Goldman knows that the cops sat back and did nothing to prevent the assassination; in fact, he criticizes them several times for precisely this. What he does not do, what he does not dare to do, is to think through *why* they sat back and to consider how those reasons tie up with both the facts and possibilities in this case. In that sense his book is irresponsible: its effect is to lessen the chances of uncovering the whole truth.

Malcolm X's high place in history is already assured; it does not depend on what is said, one way or another, about the details of his assassination. But the cause for which he gave his life requires that there be no letup in the demand for the full truth about the role of the government and the police in his assassination. It is a sign of the weakness of the current Black liberation and radical movements that they have not established an authoritative commission of inquiry to explore and report on the whole story, instead of leaving the initiative to inadequate attempts like Goldman's. Let us hope that the full story can be known and told before the coming of the revolution that will open the files of the CIA and BOSS.

7

FBI plot against the Black movement

by Baxter Smith

Proof of a vast government conspiracy to physically and politically destroy the Black movement in the U.S. has been uncovered in the most recent Watergate-related disclosures about the FBI. These disclosures reveal the hatred and fear of the rulers of this country for the Black liberation struggle as well as the ruthlessness with which they have tried to crush it.

The new facts now coming to light—including information linking the government to the murders of Malcolm X, Martin Luther King, Jr., and Fred Hampton—are prompting demands for a full public inquiry into the secret-police operations of the FBI against the Black movement. Operation PUSH leader Jesse Jackson and Congressman Ralph Metcalfe (Democrat from Illinois) have both recently urged an investigation into the government surveillance program against Blacks, which Jackson has termed "a mandate to commit murder."

The extent of this surveillance first became clear last December, when NBC newsman Carl Stern gained access to the FBI's COINTELPRO (counterintelligence program) documents. Stern won access to the files through a suit based on the Freedom of Information Act. The Socialist Workers Party and Young Socialist Alliance have also received and publicized some of the secret COINTELPRO documents through a suit they have filed against government harassment.

These documents reveal that the FBI has implemented COINTELPRO against Black groups, antiwar activists, the Socialist Workers Party, the Communist Party, and others.

Documents released March 7, 1974, present a clear picture of how COINTELPRO was set into motion against the Black movement. One memo, signed by J. Edgar Hoover and sent to FBI agents across the country, said, "The purpose of this new counterintelligence endeavor is to expose, disrupt, misdirect, discredit, or otherwise neutralize the activities of black nationalist, hate-type organizations and groupings, their leadership, spokesmen, membership, and supporters. . . ."

Dating from the period 1967 to 1970, these documents debunk the notion that illegal government surveillance and disruption began with the Nixon administration.

Never meant to be read by the American people, they reveal a coordinated, national program of repression organized in response to the Black ghetto rebellions, the Black student upsurge, and the attraction of young militants to the Black Panther Party.

One memo, dated August 25, 1967, for example, tells FBI agents to prevent Black nationalist groups from being able to "consolidate their forces or recruit new or youthful adherents. . . ." It also says that "no opportunity should be missed to exploit through counterintelligence techniques the organizational and personal conflicts of the leadership of the groups and where possible an effort should be made to capitalize upon existing conflicts between competing black nationalist organizations."

A March 4, 1968, document warns: "Prevent the *coalition* of militant black nationalist groups. In unity there is strength. . . ." The memo also urges agents to "prevent militant nationalist groups and leaders from gaining *respectability,* by discrediting them. . . ."

One document lists as a key goal: "Prevent the *rise of a 'messiah'* who could unify, and electrify, the militant black nationalist movement."

Before it turned over the documents, the FBI blotted out the names of individuals and groups listed as "targets." But it is not difficult to guess what belongs in the censored spaces. In the document on "messiahs," for example, the name of Malcolm X fits into one blanked-out area. That sentence would then read: "[Malcolm X] might have been such a 'messiah': he is the martyr of the movement today." (See appendix, p. 177.)

A following sentence might read: "[King could] be a very real contender for this position should he abandon his supposed 'obedience' to 'white, liberal doctrines' (nonviolence) and embrace black nationalism." This memo was written one month before King's murder.

Thus, as Jesse Jackson recently pointed out, these documents amount to a "search and destroy mission" against the Black movement. The killings of Malcolm X, Martin Luther King, Jr., and Fred Hampton, he explained, "were consistent with the stated purpose of the memo to prevent the rise of a messiah." And there are plenty of other indications that the government had a hand in these assassinations.

Malcolm X was the most capable Black leader of our time and greatly feared by the rulers of this country. Many questions about his murder remain unanswered.

When he was shot at a New York rally in 1965, the crowd seized two of his assailants before they could escape. The police arrested the two men and took them away, as the first newspaper reports explained. But only one of the men was ever seen again. All mention of the second man was dropped from the press without explanation, and the issue was never brought up in the trial by the court-appointed defense lawyers.

Talmadge Hayer—the man arrested at the rally and convicted— admitted his role in the assassination but refused to name his accomplices. Furthermore, he insisted that the two men convicted with him had nothing to do with the killing. This assertion gains credibility because the others convicted of the murder were known Black Muslims, and no explanation of how they could have slipped into the rally past Malcolm's security guards has ever been presented.

Although uniformed police were usually highly visible at meetings addressed by Malcolm, they were hardly in evidence the day he was shot. Malcolm himself had indicated that he considered the harassment directed against him in the last weeks of his life to be beyond the ability of any Black group to organize.

It is now known that Martin Luther King, Jr., was under intense government surveillance prior to his murder. In the spring of 1973 Arthur Murtaugh, a former FBI agent from Atlanta, revealed to the *New York Times* that J. Edgar Hoover had ordered a campaign to "get King." Wiretapping and other surveillance of the civil rights leader was so thorough that King "couldn't wiggle. They had him."

This information is all the more revealing now that James Earl Ray, the man convicted of killing King, has stated that he did not act alone. Ray says he was part of a conspiracy of white southerners. He recently filed a $500,000 damage suit against the state of Tennessee and is demanding a new trial. He says he was improperly represented by his attorney during the original trial.

The state of Tennessee, in the meantime, is trying to transfer Ray to a federal prison, where he will be isolated from the public. George McMillan, who is writing a biography of Ray, explained in the March 25, 1974, *New York Times* that under present prison regulations, "If James Earl Ray is moved into a Federal prison he will never again be able to talk face-to-face to the press, to television interviewers, or to authors of magazine articles or books."

Recent information has also come to light exposing direct FBI involvement in the 1969 raid on the Chicago apartment of Black Panther leader Fred Hampton. Hampton and another Panther leader, Mark Clark, were killed in the attack.

The *Chicago Tribune* revealed March 22, 1974, that it was the FBI that initiated the idea of the raid. First the FBI urged the Chicago police department to raid the apartment, but they refused. Then the FBI turned to State's Attorney Edward Hanrahan, who agreed to carry out the operation.

The FBI told Hanrahan's office that there was a weapons cache in Hampton's apartment, based on a report from the Panther chief of security, William O'Neal.

O'Neal was a paid FBI informer, working in COINTELPRO under FBI agent Roy Mitchell. O'Neal's undercover role in the Panthers—with its obvious implications in the Hampton case—was only discovered when he testified at the murder trial of a Black ex-cop and admitted being a spy. He has elaborated further on his role in a pretrial deposition for a suit filed by relatives of Hampton and Clark.

O'Neal was never called to the witness stand during the trial of Edward Hanrahan for obstruction of justice in the Hampton shooting, nor was it even mentioned that he had worked his way into a key post in the Panthers. The reason for this secrecy is not clear.

The Hampton-Clark murders are perhaps the most blatant of the nationwide attacks on the Black Panther Party. A chronology of those attacks indicates the development of a carefully thought-out campaign to destroy the party as it began to assume prominence in the late 1960s.

In April 1969, twenty-one Panthers were indicted in New York City on fantastic charges of conspiring to bomb department stores and subways. In December of that same year, Chicago police staged their raid on the Hampton apartment. A few days later, police in Los Angeles tried to storm a Panther headquarters. This led to a shoot-out lasting for hours in which two Panthers were wounded.

The following year, 1970, was marked by even more extensive police attacks on the Panthers. These occurred in cities such as Birmingham, Toledo, Philadelphia, New Orleans, and Detroit. At the same time, trial proceedings began against the Panther Twenty-one in New York and against Bobby Seale and Ericka Huggins in New Haven, Connecticut. These were just two of the many trials of Panthers that year.

Proof that this wave of attacks was coordinated on a national scale was revealed by the February 9, 1970, *New York Times*, which reported that Seattle Mayor Wesley Uhlman turned down a Federal proposal for a raid on Black Panther headquarters in Seattle because he did not want to popularize the Panthers' cause. He also said such raids smacked of gestapo tactics. The proposal had been made the previous month by the Alcohol, Tobacco, and Firearms Unit of the Internal Revenue Service. This outfit is now known to have been deeply involved in secret-police operations.

At the time of this concerted government campaign, the Panthers were caught up in ultraleft rhetoric, using such slogans as "off the pigs" and "pick up the gun." This only aided the government in its drive to portray the Panthers as the ones responsible for violence. It stood in the way of placing the responsibility for the violence in these attacks squarely where it belonged—on the police themselves.

Given the revelation that the Chicago Panthers' chief of security was a cop, and the discovery of agents provocateurs in other radical groups, such as the Weatherpeople and the Vietnam Veterans Against the War, it is reasonable to assume that undercover agents helped create a climate within the Panthers where the government's attacks could have maximum effect.

The experience with such agents in other groups is that they are the first to advocate terrorist actions. This stance then provides the government with a handle to discredit the left as "violent" and send radical leaders to prison.

Another police tactic used against the Panthers was revealed in a COINTELPRO memo dated May 11, 1970. It talks about fabricating documents that would appear to be "pilfered from police files," planting spies pretending to be "disgruntled police employees," and promoting factionalism by "indicating electronic coverage where none exists; outlining fictitious plans for police raids or other counteractions; revealing misuse or misappropriation of Panther funds; pointing out instances of political disorientation. . . ." (See appendix, pp. 181–82.)

Evidence that this plan did promote dissension and confusion in Panther ranks is shown by the widespread expulsions that occurred in the party around this time.

The vast scope of counterintelligence against the Panthers and other Black groups shows how terrified the government is of the power of the Black movement. In fact, when the 1970 Huston spy plan* was devised, according to the May 24, 1973, *New York Times,* "One official who worked on [it] described the most serious issue facing the Nixon Administration in mid-1970 as 'the black problem.' He said intelligence indicated that Black Panther leaders were being covertly supported by some countries in the Caribbean and in North Africa."

A study conducted by the CIA in 1969–70 disputed this alleged "foreign" connection behind the Panthers and presented a more realistic analysis of the roots of the Black upsurge in the 1960s.

One official associated with this study was quoted in the May 25, 1973, *New York Times* as saying, "We thought that it was absolutely imperative that the causes of what was happening—the Vietnam war and racial injustice—had to be understood."

War and racism were indeed the chief factors responsible for the new awakening of Blacks in the 1960s. It began with the civil rights movement and the inspiration of the Cuban revolution. There were

---

* In response to a wave of demonstrations, especially the May 1970 protests against the invasion of Cambodia and the killing of students at Kent State and Jackson State universities, White House aide Tom Charles Huston and heads of various federal spy agencies drew up a plan for intensified government attacks on dissenters, by means of burglary, spying, and mail tampering. President Nixon authorized this plan, then claimed he revoked it before implementation, because J. Edgar Hoover objected.—Ed.

explosive rebellions in the Black ghettos in the mid-60s. Then the Vietnam War, which prompted massive antiwar demonstrations, further fed the growth of Black awareness.

Lyndon "We Shall Overcome" Johnson tried to deal with the Black movement with antipoverty programs and other concessions aimed at buying off Blacks. But his strategy was two-sided, the strategy of the carrot and the stick. In his one hand, Johnson dangled the carrot of his "Great Society" programs, and in his other he held the stick of savage repression against militants that could not be bought off.

The Democrats in office before Johnson, such as John Kennedy, employed the same strategy. It was under Kennedy that a counter-intelligence program against the Socialist Workers Party was ordered in 1961. Robert Kennedy had the wiretaps on Martin Luther King, Jr., installed in 1963.

Nixon now claims that COINTELPRO has been discontinued and that the 1970 Huston spy plan never went into effect. But the harassment and intimidation of Blacks and other radicals still goes on today. Among those now in jail or facing frame-up charges are Martin Sostre, Ben Chavis, the Attica Brothers, and the Wounded Knee defendants.

Government frame-ups and the methods that go with them—undercover agents, wiretapping, and burglaries—are provoking an outcry from the American people. A growing number of victims of Watergating are fighting back, demanding a halt to these antidemocratic, illegal practices.

Relatives of Fred Hampton and Mark Clark have filed a $3.75 million lawsuit against those involved in the murderous Chicago raid. They are demanding access to FBI documents on the Chicago Panthers, and the U.S. attorney's office in Chicago has agreed to turn over "as much as a semi-truck load" of records. But it remains to be seen if the Justice Department will allow the release of the papers.

Jesse Jackson has announced plans for a class-action suit to force the disclosure of more government documents on the Black movement, and is urging other Blacks to join the suit as plaintiffs.

Congressman Ralph Metcalfe has called on the House Judiciary Committee to investigate FBI files on the Black movement. One such set of documents, called the "137" files, was maintained by the Chicago FBI on Metcalfe himself, Jesse Jackson, Southern Christian Leadership Conference leader Ralph Abernathy, and the Panthers.

The Socialist Workers Party and the Young Socialist Alliance—through their suit against bombing, burglary, and wiretapping—have already forced the government to admit that it operated an "SWP Disruption Program" from 1961 to 1969, and that it conducted electronic surveillance against the socialists beginning in 1945. The SWP and YSA suit is being publicized by the Political Rights Defense Fund.

Columnist Nat Hentoff of the *Village Voice* in New York recently secured the contents of a House Internal Security Committee (HISC) file on himself, through the help of some liberal congressmen. Among the items considered "damaging" by the House witchhunters were Hentoff's endorsements over the years of civil liberties efforts for antiwar GIs, Black Panthers, socialists, and others. Hentoff wrote in his March 7, 1974, column that he may file a suit to win the right of others to gain access to their HISC files.

There is a growing momentum in the Black community for an independent commission of inquiry into the deaths of Black leaders like Malcolm X, King, and Hampton. Jesse Jackson and others have called for this.

An inquiry into the murders could start by demanding the full truth—that the FBI turn over all files on Malcolm, King, and Hampton and other Panthers. Part of the inquiry would be to force the government to fill in those blotted-out names of FBI targets.

The impact of such an independent public inquiry was shown in the aftermath of the killing of two Black students at Southern University in Louisiana in 1972. The panel of Blacks who held hearings on the shootings proved that the cops had deliberately fired on defenseless demonstrators.

In a similar fashion, an inquiry into the deaths of Malcolm, King, and Hampton could present the truth to a wide audience. Such an inquiry should be organized by, and responsible to, the Black community. The Democrats and Republicans in Washington and their "special prosecutors" have shown no interest in investigating the Watergate-type crimes against Blacks—and no wonder, since those crimes have been committed under both Democratic and Republican administrations.

What Watergate has shown is the hard-nosed determination of the rulers of this country to prevent the spread of independent struggles of Black people. They do not stop at anything, including murder.

But their secret-police tactics have been put in the spotlight for all to see. The government is on the defensive around these exposures and now is the time to press further.

The opportunity has never been greater to force a halt to these illegal attacks, to expose the lack of democracy in this country, and to show where the responsibility for violence in this society really lies.

To the extent that Blacks take advantage of this opportunity and win victories against these repressive measures, the struggle to end racial oppression and all other forms of exploitation in the U.S. will take a step forward.

APPENDIX

SECRET FBI MEMOS ON THE BLACK MOVEMENT

The documents reproduced here were released by the FBI as a result of a lawsuit filed by Carl Stern, a reporter for NBC, under the Freedom of Information Act.

The photocopies released by the government contain some passages that have been blotted out with a dark marking pen, and other sections covered over by paper apparently attached with paper clips.

SAC, Albany

August 25, 1967

Director, FBI

COUNTERINTELLIGENCE PROGRAM
BLACK NATIONALIST - HATE GROUPS
INTERNAL SECURITY

Offices receiving copies of this letter are instructed
to immediately establish a control file, captioned as above, and
to assign responsibility for following and coordinating this new
counterintelligence program to an experienced and imaginative
Special Agent well versed in investigations relating to black
nationalist, hate-type organizations. The field office control
file used under this program may be maintained in a pending
inactive status until such time as a specific operation or
technique is placed under consideration for implementation.

The purpose of this new counterintelligence endeavor
is to expose, disrupt, misdirect, discredit, or otherwise
neutralize the activities of black nationalist, hate-type
organizations and groupings, their leadership, spokesmen,
membership, and supporters, and to counter their propensity for
violence and civil disorder. The activities of all such groups
of intelligence interest to this Bureau must be followed on a
continuous basis so we will be in a position to promptly take
advantage of all opportunities for counterintelligence and to
inspire action in instances where circumstances warrant. The
pernicious background of such groups, their duplicity, and devious
maneuvers must be exposed to public scrutiny where such publicity
will have a neutralizing effect. Efforts of the various groups/

Letter to SAC, Albany
RE: COUNTERINTELLIGENCE PROGRAM
    BLACK NATIONALIST - HATE GROUPS

to consolidate their forces or to recruit new or youthful
adherents must be frustrated. No opportunity should be missed
to exploit through counterintelligence techniques the
organizational and personal conflicts of the leaderships of the
groups and where possible an effort should be made to capitalize
upon existing conflicts between competing black nationalist
organizations. When an opportunity is apparent to disrupt or
neutralize black nationalist, hate-type organizations through the
cooperation of established local news media contacts or through
such contact with sources available to the Seat of Government,
in every instance careful attention must be given to the proposal
to insure the targeted group is disrupted, ridiculed, or
discredited through the publicity and not merely publicized.
Consideration should be given to techniques to preclude violence-
prone or rabble-rouser leaders of hate groups from spreading their
philosophy publicly or through various mass communication media.

        Many individuals currently active in black nationalist
organizations have backgrounds of immorality, subversive activity,
and criminal records. Through your investigation of key agitators
you should endeavor to establish their unsavory backgrounds.
Be alert to determine evidence of misappropriation of funds or
other types of personal misconduct on the part of militant
nationalist leaders so any practical or warranted counterintelligence may be instituted.

        Intensified attention under this program should be
afforded to the activities of such groups as the

_____ Particular emphasis should be given to
extremists who direct the activities and policies of
revolutionary or militant groups such as

        At this time the Bureau is setting up no requirement
for status letters to be periodically submitted under this
program. It will be incumbent upon you to insure the program
is being afforded necessary and continuing attention and that
no opportunities will be overlooked for counterintelligence
action.

        This program should not be confused with the program
entitled "Communist Party, USA, Counterintelligence Program,
Internal Security - C," _____, which is directed

-2-

against the Communist Party and related organizations, or the program entitled "Counterintelligence Program, Internal Security, Disruption of Hate Groups," (＿＿＿＿＿＿), which is directed against Klan and hate-type groups primarily consisting of white memberships.

All Special Agent personnel responsible for the investigation of black nationalist, hate-type organizations and their memberships should be alerted to our counterintelligence interest and each investigative Agent has a responsibility to call to the attention of the counterintelligence coordinator suggestions and possibilities for implementing the program. You are also cautioned that the nature of this new endeavor is such that under no circumstances should the existence of the program be made known outside the Bureau and appropriate within-office security should be afforded to sensitive operations and techniques considered under the program.

No counterintelligence action under this program may be initiated by the field without specific prior Bureau authorization.

You are urged to take an enthusiastic and imaginative approach to this new counterintelligence endeavor and the Bureau will be pleased to entertain any suggestions or techniques you may recommend.

Date: 3/4/68

The following in _____
              (Type in plaintext or code)

AIRTEL
                            (Priority)

To: SAC, Albany   PERSONAL ATTENTION

From: Director, FBI

COUNTERINTELLIGENCE PROGRAM
BLACK NATIONALIST-HATE GROUPS
RACIAL INTELLIGENCE

      Title is changed to substitute Racial Intelligence
for Internal Security for Bureau routing purposes.

Sent Via _____ M   Per ____

BACKGROUND

By letter dated 8/25/67 the following offices
were advised of the beginning of a Counterintelligence
Program against militant Black Nationalist-Hate Groups:

Each of the above offices was to designate a
Special Agent to coordinate this program. Replies to this
letter indicated an interest in counterintelligence against
militant black nationalist groups that foment violence and
several offices outlined procedures which had been effective
in the past. For example, █████████████████████
furnished information about a new ████████████████
grade school to appropriate authorities in ████████████
████████████ who investigated to determine if the school
conformed to █████████████████ for private schools. █████
████████████ obtained background information on the parents
of each pupil.

The ████████████████████████████
████████████████████ group, was active in
in the summer of 1957. ████████████████████████ alerted
local police, who then put █████ leaders under close scrutiny.
They were arrested on every possible charge until they could
no longer make bail. As a result, █████ leaders spent most of the
summer in jail and no violence traceable to █████ took place.

The Counterintelligence Program is now being
expanded to include 41 offices. Each of the offices added
to this program should designate an Agent familiar with black

- 2 -

nationalist activity, and interested in counterintelligence, to coordinate this program. This Agent will be responsible for the periodic progress letters being requested, but each Agent working this type of case should participate in the formulation of counterintelligence operations.

GOALS

For maximum effectiveness of the Counterintelligence Program, and to prevent wasted effort, long-range goals are being set.

1. Prevent the coalition of militant black nationalist groups. In unity there is strength; a truism that is no less valid for all its triteness. An effective coalition of black nationalist groups might be the first step toward a real "Mau Mau" in America, the beginning of a true black revolution.

2. Prevent the rise of a "messiah" who could unify, and electrify, the militant black nationalist movement. ⬛⬛⬛⬛⬛ might have been such a "messiah;" he is the martyr of the movement today. ⬛⬛⬛⬛⬛⬛⬛⬛ all aspire to this position. ⬛⬛⬛⬛⬛ is less of a threat because of his age. ⬛⬛⬛⬛⬛ could be a very real contender for this position should he abandon his supposed "obedience" to "white, liberal doctrines" (nonviolence) and embrace black nationalism. ⬛⬛⬛⬛⬛⬛ has the necessary charisma to be a real threat in this way.

3. Prevent violence on the part of black nationalist groups. This is of primary importance, and is, of course, a goal of our investigative activity; it should also be a goal of the Counterintelligence Program. Through counterintelligence it should be possible to pinpoint potential troublemakers and neutralize them before they exercise their potential for violence.

4. Prevent militant black nationalist groups and leaders from gaining respectability, by discrediting them to three separate segments of the community. The goal of discrediting black nationalists must be handled tactically in three ways. You must discredit these groups and individuals to, first, the responsible Negro community. Second, they must be discredited to the white community,

- 3 -

both the responsible community and to "liberals" who have vestiges of sympathy for militant black nationalist simply because they are Negroes. Third, these groups must be discredited in the eyes of Negro radicals, the followers of the movement. This last area requires entirely different tactics from the first two. Publicity about violent tendencies and radical statements merely enhances black nationalists to the last group; it adds "respectability" in a different way.

5. A final goal should be to prevent the long-range growth of militant black nationalist organizations, especially among youth. Specific tactics to prevent these groups from converting young people must be developed.

Besides these five goals counterintelligence is a valuable part of our regular investigative program as it often produces positive information.

TARGETS

Primary targets of the Counterintelligence Program, Black Nationalist-Hate Groups, should be the most violent and radical groups and their leaders. We should emphasize those leaders and organizations that are nationwide in scope and are most capable of disrupting this country. These targets should include the radical and violence-prone leaders, members, and followers of the:

Offices handling these cases and those of should be alert for counterintelligence suggestions.

INSTRUCTIONS

Within 30 days of the date of this letter each office should:

1. Advise the Bureau of the identity of the Special Agent assigned to coordinate this program.

- 4 -

2. Submit a very succinct summary of the black nationalist movement in the field office territory. Include name, number of members and degree of activity of each black nationalist group. Also state your estimate of each group's propensity for violence. This is for target evaluation only, not for record purposes. Second, list Rabble-Rouser Index subjects who are militant black nationalists and any other militant black nationalist leaders who might be future targets of counterintelligence action because of their propensity for violence. Include a minimum of background information on each person listed; a few descriptive sentences should suffice.

3. List those organizations and individuals you consider of such potential danger as to be considered for current counterintelligence action. Briefly justify each target.

4. Submit any suggestion you have for overall counterintelligence action or the administration of this program. Suggestions for action against any specific target should be submitted by separate letter.

5. Submit, by separate letter, suggestions for counterintelligence action against the targets previously listed as field-wide. These should not be general, such as "publicize ⟨⟨⟨⟨⟨⟨⟩⟩⟩⟩⟩ to communist countries," but should be specific as to target, what is to be done, what contacts are to be used, and all other information needed for the Bureau to approve a counterintelligence operation.

Thereafter, on a ninety-day basis, each office is to submit a progress letter summarizing counterintelligence operations proposed during the period, operations effected, and tangible results. Any changes in the overall black nationalist movement should be summarized in this letter. This should include new organizations, new leaders, and any changes in data listed under number two above. Suggestions for counterintelligence operations should not be set out in this progress letter. Use the following captions:

1. Operations Under Consideration, 2. Operations Being Effected, 3. Tangible Results, and 4. Developments of Counterintelligence Interest. These 90-day progress letters are due at the Bureau the first day of March, June, September, and December, excepting March, 1968.

- 5 -

The effectiveness of counterintelligence depends
on the quality and quantity of positive information
available regarding the target and on the imagination and
initiative of Agents working the program. The response <u>of</u>
the field to the Counterintelligence Program against the
Communist Party, USA, indicates that a superb job can be
done by the field on counterintelligence.

Counterintelligence operations must be approved
by the Bureau. Because of the nature of this program each
operation must be designed to protect the Bureau's interest
so that there is no possibility of embarrassment to the
Bureau. Beyond this the Bureau will give every possible
consideration to your proposals.

SAC, San Francisco   5/11/70

Director, FBI

COUNTERINTELLIGENCE AND SPECIAL OPERATIONS
(RESEARCH SECTION)

        The Bureau would like to offer for your consideration
a proposal for a disruptive-disinformation operation targeted
against the national office of the Black Panther Party (BPP).
This proposal is not intended to be all inclusive or binding
in any of its various phases, but only is a guide for the
suggested action. You are encouraged to submit recommendations
relating to revisions or innovations of the proposal.

        1. The operation would be effected through close
coordination on a high level with the Oakland or San Francisco
Police Department.

        2. Xerox copies of true documents, documents subtly
incorporating false information, and entirely fabricated documents
would be periodically anonymously mailed to the residence of a
key Panther leader. These documents would be on the stationery
and in the form used by the police department or by the FBI in
disseminating information to the police. FBI documents, when
used, would contain police routing or date received notations,
clearly indicating they had been pilfered from police files.

        3. An attempt would be made to give the Panther
recipient the impression the documents were stolen from police
files by a disgruntled police employee sympathetic to the
Panthers. After initial mailings, brief notes by the alleged
disgruntled employee would be included with the mailed documents.
These notes would indicate the motive and sympathy of the police
employee, his bitterness against his department, and possibly
a request for money

        4. Depending on developments, at a propitious time,
consideration would be given to establishing a post office box
or other suitable "drop" address for the use of the alleged
disgruntled employee to receive responses, funds, and/or
specifications relating to the documents from the Panthers.

5. Although the operation may not require inclusion of a live source to represent the disgruntled employee, circumstances might warrant the use of such a source for face-to-face meetings with the Panthers. During early stages of the operation, an effort should be made to locate and brief a suitable police employee to play the role of the alleged disgruntled employee.

6. A wide variety of alleged authentic police or FBI material could be carefully selected or prepared for furnishing to the Panthers. Reports, blind memoranda, LHMs, and other alleged police or FBI documents could be prepared pinpointing Panthers as police or FBI informants; ridiculing or discrediting Panther leaders through their ineptness or personal escapades; espousing personal philosophies and promoting factionalism among BPP members; indicating electronic coverage where none exists; outlining fictitious plans for police raids or other counteractions; revealing misuse or misappropriation of Panther funds; pointing out instances of political disorientation; etc. The nature of the disruptive material and disinformation "leaked" would only be limited by the collection ability of your sources and the need to insure the protection of their security.

Effective implementation of this proposal logically could not help but disrupt and confuse Panther activities. Even if they were to suspect FBI or police involvement, they would be unable to ignore factual material brought to their attention through this channel. The operation would afford us a continuing means to furnish the Panther leadership true information which is to our interest that they know and disinformation which, in their interest, they may not ignore.

Although this proposal is a relatively simple technique, it has been applied with exceptional results in another area of intelligence interest where the target was of far greater sophistication. The Bureau believes with careful planning this technique has excellent long-range potential to disrupt and curtail Panther activity.

- 2 -

·SAC, San Francisco   4/2/69

Director, FBI

COUNTERINTELLIGENCE AND SPECIAL OPERATIONS
(NATIONALITIES INTELLIGENCE)

_____ReSFairtel 3/26/69 under dual caption of
_____ and _____
suggesting disruptive action relating to the two organizations.

                Reairtel designated copies for the Bufile
and the SFfile   on "Cointelpro - New Left."

                There is no objection to your action, but you are
reminded of the existence of the captioned case file which
may be used for a broad range of disruptive activity and
which has a specific interest in techniques and operations
in the pro-Chicom area.

INDEX

The fight for Black freedom

Fighting Racism in World War II

C.L.R. James, George Breitman, Edgar Keemer, and others

A week-by-week account of the struggle against racism and racial discrimination in the United States from 1939 to 1945, taken from the pages of the socialist newsweekly, the *Militant*. $22

Cointelpro

THE FBI'S SECRET WAR ON POLITICAL FREEDOM

Nelson Blackstock

Describes the decades-long covert counterintelligence program—code-named Cointelpro—directed against socialists and activists in the Black and anti-Vietnam War movements. The operations revealed in the documents cited in this book—many of them photographically reproduced—provide an unprecedented look at the methods used by the FBI, CIA, military intelligence, and other U.S. police agencies. Despite their authors' intentions, these documents also record pieces of the history of efforts to build the communist movement in the United States. $16

Marx and Engels on the United States

Karl Marx and Frederick Engels

Articles and letters from 1846 to 1895 examine the rise of U.S. capitalism, the historic conflict with a system based on slave labor, the impact of the frontier and free land, and the challenges facing the emerging working-class movement. Indispensable for understanding the economic roots and consequences of the Civil War and the class structure and conflicts of the United States today. $15.95

Leon Trotsky on Black Nationalism and Self-Determination

Drawing on lessons from the October 1917 Russian revolution, Trotsky explains why uncompromising opposition to racial discrimination and support to Blacks' struggle for national self-determination are an essential part of the strategy to unite the working class to make a socialist revolution in the United States. $13

The First and Second Declarations of Havana

Nowhere are the questions of revolutionary strategy that today confront men and women on the front lines of struggles in the Americas addressed with greater truthfulness and clarity than in these uncompromising indictments of imperialist plunder and "the exploitation of man by man." Adopted by million-strong assemblies of the Cuban people in 1960 and 1962. $10. Also in Spanish.

Our History Is Still Being Written

The Story of Three Chinese–Cuban Generals in the Cuban Revolution

Armando Choy, Gustavo Chui, and Moisés Sío Wong talk about the historic place of Chinese immigration to Cuba, as well as over five decades of revolutionary action and internationalism, from Cuba to Angola and Venezuela today. Through their stories we see the social and political forces that gave birth to the Cuban nation and opened the door to socialist revolution in the Americas. $20. Also in Spanish.

To Speak the Truth

Why Washington's 'Cold War' against Cuba Doesn't End

FIDEL CASTRO, ERNESTO CHE GUEVARA

In historic speeches before the United Nations and UN bodies, Guevara and Castro address the peoples of the world, explaining why the U.S. government so fears the example set by the socialist revolution in Cuba and why Washington's effort to destroy it will fail. $17

Cuba and the Coming American Revolution

JACK BARNES

This is a book about prospects for revolution in the United States, where the political capacities of workers and farmers are today as utterly discounted by the ruling powers as were those of the Cuban toilers. It is about the example set by the people of Cuba that revolution is not only necessary—it can be made. Second edition, with new foreword by Mary-Alice Waters. $13. Also in Spanish and French.

Che Guevara Talks to Young People

ERNESTO CHE GUEVARA

In eight talks from 1959 to 1964, the Argentine-born revolutionary challenges youth of Cuba and the world to study, to work, to become disciplined. To join the front lines of struggles, small and large. To politicize their organizations and themselves. To become a different kind of human being as they strive together with working people of all lands to transform the world. $15. Also in Spanish.

Playa Girón/Bay of Pigs

Washington's First Military Defeat in the Americas
FIDEL CASTRO, JOSÉ RAMÓN FERNÁNDEZ

In fewer than 72 hours of combat in April 1961, Cuba's revolutionary armed forces defeated a U.S.-organized invasion by 1,500 mercenaries. In the process, the Cuban people set an example for workers, farmers, and youth the world over that with political consciousness, class solidarity, courage, and revolutionary leadership, one can stand up to enormous might and seemingly insurmountable odds—and win. $20. Also in Spanish.

Dynamics of the Cuban Revolution

A Marxist Appreciation
JOSEPH HANSEN

How did the Cuban Revolution unfold? Why does it represent an "unbearable challenge" to U.S. imperialism? What political obstacles has it overcome? Written as the revolution advanced from its earliest days. $25

Also from
PATHFINDER

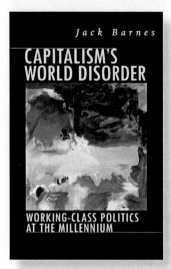

Capitalism's World Disorder
Working-Class Politics at the Millennium
JACK BARNES

The social devastation and financial panic, the coarsening of politics, the cop brutality and acts of imperialist aggression accelerating around us—all are the product not of something gone wrong with capitalism but of its lawful workings. Yet the future can be changed by the united struggle and selfless action of workers and farmers conscious of their power to transform the world. $24. Also in Spanish and French.

The Changing Face of U.S. Politics
Working-Class Politics and the Trade Unions
JACK BARNES

Building the kind of party working people need to prepare for coming class battles through which they will organize and strengthen the unions, as they revolutionize themselves and all society. A handbook for those repelled by the class inequalities, racism, women's oppression, cop violence, and wars inherent in capitalism, for those who are seeking the road toward effective action to overturn that exploitative system and join in reconstructing the world on new, socialist foundations. $23. Also in Spanish, French and Swedish.

The Communist Manifesto
KARL MARX AND FREDERICK ENGELS

Founding document of the modern working-class movement, published in 1848. Explains why communism is not a set of preconceived principles but the line of march of the working class toward power, "springing from an existing class struggle, a historical movement going on under our very eyes." $4. Also in Spanish.

www.pathfinderpress.com

Teamster Rebellion
FARRELL DOBBS

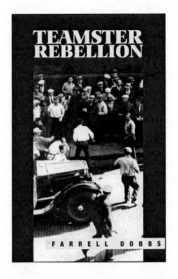

The 1934 strikes that built the industrial union movement in Minneapolis and helped pave the way for the CIO, recounted by a central leader of that battle. The first in a four-volume series on the class-struggle leadership of the strikes and organizing drives that transformed the Teamsters union in much of the Midwest into a fighting social movement and pointed the road toward independent labor political action. $19. Also in Spanish.

Cosmetics, Fashions, and the Exploitation of Women
JOSEPH HANSEN, EVELYN REED, AND MARY-ALICE WATERS

How big business plays on women's second-class status and social insecurities to market cosmetics and rake in profits. The introduction by Waters explains how the entry of millions of women into the workforce during and after World War II irreversibly changed U.S. society and laid the basis for a renewed rise of struggles for women's emancipation. $15

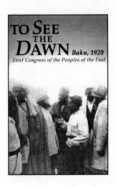

To See the Dawn
Baku, 1920—First Congress of the Peoples of the East

How can peasants and workers in the colonial world achieve freedom from imperialist exploitation? By what means can working people overcome divisions incited by their national ruling classes and act together for their common class interests? These questions were addressed by 2,000 delegates to the 1920 Congress of the Peoples of the East. $22

The Jewish Question
A Marxist Interpretation
ABRAM LEON

Traces the historical rationalizations of anti-Semitism to the fact that, in the centuries preceding the domination of industrial capitalism, Jews emerged as a "people-class" of merchants, moneylenders, and traders. Leon explains why the propertied rulers incite renewed Jew-hatred in the epoch of capitalism's decline. $20

www.pathfinderpress.com

New International

A MAGAZINE OF MARXIST POLITICS AND THEORY

NEW INTERNATIONAL NO. 12

CAPITALISM'S LONG HOT WINTER HAS BEGUN

Jack Barnes

and "Their Transformation and Ours," Resolution of the Socialist Workers Party

Today's sharpening interimperialist conflicts are fueled both by the opening stages of what will be decades of economic, financial, and social convulsions and class battles, and by the most far-reaching shift in Washington's military policy and organization since the U.S. buildup toward World War II. Class-struggle-minded working people must face this historic turning point for imperialism, and draw satisfaction from being "in their face" as we chart a revolutionary course to confront it. $16

NEW INTERNATIONAL NO. 13

OUR POLITICS START WITH THE WORLD

Jack Barnes

The huge economic and cultural inequalities between imperialist and semicolonial countries, and among classes within almost every country, are produced, re-produced, and accentuated by the workings of capital-ism. For vanguard workers to build parties able to lead a successful revolutionary struggle for power in our own countries, says Jack Barnes in the lead article, our activity must be guided by a strategy to close this gap.

Also includes: "Farming, Science, and the Working Classes" *by Steve Clark* and "Capitalism, Labor, and Nature: An Exchange" *by Richard Levins, Steve Clark.* $14

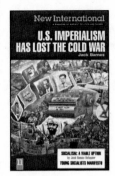

NEW INTERNATIONAL NO. 11
U.S. IMPERIALISM HAS LOST THE COLD WAR

Jack Barnes

Contrary to imperialist expectations at the opening of the 1990s in the wake of the collapse of regimes across Eastern Europe and the USSR claiming to be communist, the workers and farmers there have not been crushed. Nor have capitalist social relations been stabilized. The toilers remain an intractable obstacle to imperialism's advance, one the exploiters will have to confront in class battles and war. $16

NEW INTERNATIONAL NO. 10
IMPERIALISM'S MARCH TOWARD FASCISM AND WAR

Jack Barnes

"There will be new Hitlers, new Mussolinis. That is inevitable. What is not inevitable is that they will triumph. The working-class vanguard will organize our class to fight back against the devastating toll we are made to pay for the capitalist crisis. The future of humanity will be decided in the contest between these contending class forces." $16

NEW INTERNATIONAL NO. 8
CHE GUEVARA, CUBA, AND THE ROAD TO SOCIALISM

Articles by Ernesto Che Guevara, Carlos Rafael Rodríguez, Carlos Tablada, Mary-Alice Waters, Steve Clark, Jack Barnes

Exchanges from the opening years of the Cuban Revolution and today on the political perspectives defended by Guevara as he helped lead working people to advance the transformation of economic and social relations in Cuba. $10

NEW INTERNATIONAL NO. 7
OPENING GUNS OF WORLD WAR III: WASHINGTON'S ASSAULT ON IRAQ

Jack Barnes

The murderous assault on Iraq in 1990–91 heralded increasingly sharp conflicts among imperialist powers, growing instability of international capitalism, and more wars. *Also includes:* "1945: When U.S. Troops said 'No!'" *by Mary-Alice Waters* and "Lessons from the Iran-Iraq War" *by Samad Sharif.* $14

PATHFINDER AROUND THE WORLD

Visit our website for a complete list of titles and to place orders

www.pathfinderpress.com

PATHFINDER DISTRIBUTORS

UNITED STATES
(and Caribbean, Latin America, and East Asia)

> *Pathfinder Books, 306 W. 37th St., 10th Floor,*
> *New York, NY 10018*

CANADA

> *Pathfinder Books, 2238 Dundas St. West, Suite 201,*
> *Toronto, ON M6R 3A9*

UNITED KINGDOM
(and Europe, Africa, Middle East, and South Asia)

> *Pathfinder Books, First Floor, 120 Bethnal Green Road*
> *(entrance in Brick Lane), London E2 6DG*

SWEDEN

> *Pathfinder böcker, Bildhuggarvägen 17, S-121 44 Johanneshov*

AUSTRALIA
(and Southeast Asia and the Pacific)

> *Pathfinder, Level 1, 3/281-287 Beamish St., Campsie, NSW 2194*
> *Postal address: P.O. Box 164, Campsie, NSW 2194*

NEW ZEALAND

> *Pathfinder, 7 Mason Ave. (upstairs), Otahuhu, Auckland*
> *Postal address: P.O. Box 3025, Auckland 1140*